BEEF JOHNSTON

GOLF IS HARD

HarperCollins*Publishers*

HarperCollins*Publishers*
1 London Bridge Street
London SE1 9GF

www.harpercollins.co.uk

HarperCollins*Publishers*
Macken House, 39/40 Mayor Street Upper
Dublin 1, D01 C9W8, Ireland

First published by HarperCollins*Publishers* 2024
This edition published 2025

1 3 5 7 9 10 8 6 4 2

A catalogue record of this book is
available from the British Library

ISBN 978-0-00-866339-1

Printed and bound in the UK using 100%
renewable electricity at CPI Group (UK) Ltd

To Jodie and Harley

CONTENTS

1

WHY GOLF?

Things are really looking up. I'm in Switzerland, playing at Crans-sur-Sierre. It's a quirky little course that suits my game down to the ground, and I need that right now. I've been out injured for ages, I need to impress. I need to get some points on the board, or I'm in danger of losing my tour card.

I've made a good start, though. I've made the cut. I've parred the first two holes. And now there's a par three where I can pick up a birdie. Or perhaps even better …

It's a tricky one, though. The pin is at the back of the green and there's a little ledge just behind it where it drops away. It's dangerous. Best to play it safe and just drop it in the middle of the green.

I take out my seven iron and set myself up. I take a breath, address the ball, draw back the club … and I swing. THWOCK! There's a good connection, the ball rises up into the air and I watch as it bounces hard on the green … and rolls straight off it to the right. Shit.

I walk down to assess the damage. It's bad. It's an impossible chip shot. All I can do is give it a bit of bump and run, and hope it ends up in the right place. Maybe I can salvage a par.

It does *not* end up in the right place. I hit it too hard and it zips across the green and off the other side into the rough. Fuck. But at least this time, I can chip it. And so I chip it. Straight over the fucking green and right back where I put it from the tee shot. I walk over, shaking my head in silent fury at myself. That's three shots already. Even if I fluke it in from here, it's a bogey.

But I don't fluke it in. I go for the bump and run again. I try to take a bit of pace off it, but I hit the fucking thing straight across the green and out into the rough again. That's four. Another chip shot. Another shit shot. I've put too much on it, miss the green and I am back in that spot for the third fucking time. Five.

My head's gone now. Never mind a good finish, never mind impressing anyone. I've tried to make a good start and climb up the leaderboard, but I've nearly fallen off it.

There's a crowd here, about 50 or 60 people, and they're not saying a word. They just stand silently and watch me as I repeatedly twat the ball back and forth across the green. Mercifully, the next attempt hits the green and stays there. I miss the first putt and drop it in with the second to make an *eight*.

I am past the point of being angry. I am somewhere else now. It's all just so fucking ridiculous. I pick the ball out of the hole, put it in my pocket and shout, 'Fifteen love!' at the crowd. They fall about laughing. I join in. At a time like that, there's nothing else you can do.

Sometimes people see moments like that and they say, 'You're a professional golfer – how can it go that badly wrong?'

The answer is that it's just not that easy. Golf is hard. It's not a video game. You don't just hit the ball perfectly every single time. It's a constant battle. A battle against the course, against the elements and against yourself. And even professional golfers hit bad shots. I guess that's why it's such an addictive sport, and why it holds people like you and me in its grip. Because no matter how bad a day you've had out there, you always come back, don't you? You always want to be better next time..

People wonder sometimes how I ended up playing golf. And I don't blame them. My dad was a bus driver, my mum was a dinner lady. I'm not exactly the country club type.

They wonder what it is about the sport that attracts a working-class boy from Finchley. Why he wouldn't go for football or cricket or boxing.

Well, let me tell you what I love most about golf.

It's those early mornings. Those early summer mornings when you get to the golf course first thing. You know the ones. It's 7 a.m., there's hardly anyone there, the course is untouched. It's perfect.

You turn up, you grab a bacon roll, and then you just get out there and you start hitting golf balls.

It's so early that you've still got dew on the course. The greens are still wet and you've got that smell of cut grass in the air.

Sometimes you can hear traffic in the background and you think, 'They're all going to work. But *this* is my work. Oh man, I'm on the golf course.'

It's all sitting there waiting for you: this golfing paradise. And that's why I love golf. Just being out there.

And that's just when I'm practising or playing with my mates. It's even better on a tournament day when you're playing well and you feel like you're on a roll. You just think: this is it. This is incredible.

This is one hundred per cent the best thing ever. When I look back at some of the moments I've had, some of the places golf has taken me … I'm blessed.

I've had real jobs too. I've been a labourer on building sites. That was tough. When you work with people who've done that sort of thing for a long time and they're used to the slog, well, stepping into their world was a real eye-opener.

I worked on a renovation job once, this massive place, and we took a delivery of fifty or so heavy fire doors. Well, I say 'we'. When the doors showed up, everyone else had mysteriously vanished. I had to take them all off the lorry myself. Off the lorry and up the stairs. I remember finishing that day and just thinking, 'Fucking hell. This is brutal, man.' I was done. Straight home, dinner, bed. Done.

So I know how lucky I am.

Also, if you're going to play any sport professionally, wouldn't you pick golf? I love my boxing, but at least when I have a bad day at work, I just go back to the club-house, have a chat with my coach and then try to do better next time. If you have a bad day at work when you're a boxer, you get the shit kicked out of you.

My dad drove buses for a long time and then he worked in a timber yard. My mum was out there every day, serving lunch at my primary school. They worked so hard for the family, me, my brother and my sister. I had an amazing childhood and I wouldn't change it for the world. I was lucky. People talk about privilege and coming from money, but I don't know if there's a better privilege in this life than having two parents who love you and will do anything for you.

They got me into sport too. We played everything in our family: football, cricket, tennis, table tennis. My dad was sports mad and he'd watch anything. But it was always golf that I kept coming back to. I just loved it.

Even at the age of four, I was swinging golf clubs out in the back garden. Dad used to take me over to the local playing fields and we'd just whack a load of balls all morning. And then he took me to my first pitch and putt.

Now, you've got to remember that I'm four years old at this time. I've got sawn-off golf clubs. I'm too small for proper clubs and we haven't got the money for those specially made children's ones, so my dad's cut a seven iron and a wedge down for me with a hacksaw.

I think the reason I swing the club like I do was because of those bigger clubs I used when I was a kid. I'd sort of pick up the club and rotate my wrists hard to try to build up the momentum to get it going. Almost as if I was winding myself up like a clockwork toy.

And I remember going to that pitch and putt course, Grovelands in Southgate, north London, and the staff weren't having any of it.

They said to my dad, 'No, mate. He can't play. Look at him! He's not big enough!'

And my dad turned around and said, 'You just watch him hit one.'

Now I'm four years old, I don't have a fucking clue what's going on most of the time, but even when you're that age, you know what it means when someone says, 'You just watch him hit one.' You're under pressure. The adrenaline starts flowing. It's time to deliver.

I stepped up, took a big swing and I smacked it straight down the course and the staff were all, like, 'Yeah, fair enough. He can play.'

I wonder sometimes if my dad was shitting it that day, thinking, 'Don't embarrass me, kid. Don't embarrass me.'

But that was it. I was off. We used to go a lot back then, on the weekends and through the summer. We played three or four times a day, just going round and round and round. I never wanted to go home. I did play other sports, but golf just kept dragging me back. I'd be away on a football camp over the summer and I'd be thinking, 'I just want to play golf now.'

I wish I could tell you what it was that made me fall in love with the sport. Was it the way I felt when I hit a ball just right and it split the fairway? Maybe. Was it how I felt when I backed myself to take a risk and it paid off? A bit. But mostly I think it was just going out and spending time with my friends. Spending time with my dad.

Oh, and as for all that country club stuff, the truth is that golf isn't really a sport for the elite. Or at least it doesn't have to be. My golf club isn't like that at all. It's mostly working class. It's builders and cab drivers, and I think a lot of clubs around the country are similar.

A good golf club is like a little community. When I was young, I never felt that class was a blocker for me at North Middlesex, or North Mid as we call it. We used to go up and play golf, hang out at the club, mess around. It was a good bunch of people up there. You didn't have to worry if you weren't wearing the right kind of socks or anything like that.

I saw a bit of that when I was coming up through the junior levels with boys from the same background, like Tommy Fleetwood or Eddie Pepperell, playing at golf clubs where you had to wear a suit to get in. When it all goes a bit proper, I usually struggle a bit. I'm like, 'Oh fuck, do I have to wear a suit for this one? Just let me hit golf balls.'

Don't get me wrong, I loved pulling on the shirt and representing England and all that. But the suits and the fancy dinners just did my fucking head in.

But this was nearly 20 years ago now. Golf is changing and you don't get so much of that. Look at the clothes that they're making these days. Puma are making golf *hoodies*. The golf shoes now look like trainers. I'm happiest playing in jogging bottoms, I just want the comfort.

And, partly because things are starting to relax, you're seeing more and more people getting into the game. Another thing was Covid.

The number of times I'm speaking to people about why they got into golf and they say that it was Covid that did it.

The pandemic was awful, but it did golf a massive favour because it was one of the few things you could do when we were coming out of lockdown. People had been stuck indoors for ages and they thought, 'Well, why not?' And once they get hooked, they stay hooked.

Before the pandemic, loads of golf courses were struggling and now they're really busy. Once people start playing and they get into it, once they understand it and realise that it's basically just three or four hours out with their mates, they're in for life. I try to get back to my local course as often as I can and the last time I was up there, I've come in, I'm looking around and I'm thinking, 'There's so many new faces here! I don't recognise any of these people.' It's amazing and it's all because of Covid. They've come in, they've picked up a club, they've got out there and then it hits them; they realise what they've been missing.

It's not *just* Covid, though. I think a lot of people started playing because they realised how long they were spending staring at screens. Before the pandemic, people would be waking up, staring at their phone, getting on the train, staring at their phone, getting to work, staring at a screen, getting on the train, staring at their phone, off to bed and then it's the same thing all over again the next day.

I'm terrible with it sometimes. You pick up your phone because it buzzes and then you find yourself sat there 30 minutes later, scrolling down a timeline and you're like, 'How's that happened to me again?!'

Phones are such a distraction. They're not banned at my club, but they're definitely not welcomed by me. If it was down to me, it would be a case of 'Put your phone away, stick it in your bag, leave it in your bag. Go and play!'

If anyone gets their phone out and takes a call when I'm playing, I'll just leave them to it. I'm not waiting around. I'm off. You're the one who's missing out.

Go be with your mates, have a laugh with your mates. Look around at where you are and soak it all up. It's so good for the mind and the soul. You're playing a game, you want to improve, you want to win, you want to beat your mates, but it's golf. Enjoy it. Have a laugh, have a good time.

And on the golf course you can play with your mates in a way you can't with any other sport. In fact, if you can swing a club and hit a ball, more often than not you can play with anyone. I couldn't play five-a-side football with Lionel Messi, but with the handicap system, any halfway competent golfer can play, on an even playing field, with any professional.

A couple of weeks before I started this book, I played a round with my podcast co-host John Robins. He's a comedian, he's never been a professional sportsman of any kind, but if I give him an extra shot every hole, our games are pretty tight. In fact, last time we played nine holes he beat me, and he's never stopped talking about it. That's one of my favourite things about this sport.

So how do you get from absolute beginner to halfway competent? I think lessons are key. I'll tell you some of the technical stuff in this book, I'll try to give you a few tips, but actual lessons are so key for beginners because you need to get into good habits.

The starting point of golf, the very first thing you'll ever do, is grip your club. If you hold it badly, you're going to be struggling forever. I've seen it so many times. I've seen people holding the club and I've thought, 'Oh my God, how is he going to hit that?'

If you can get into good habits at the start, it will really pay off later down the line. You don't need to get some super coach, an old pro charging stupid money. You just need someone decent who will teach you the basics.

And that includes the swing. The swing is weird. It's not a normal move for a human to make. Some people find it really difficult.

When I've taught beginners, I've just tried to get them to sit up, grip properly and literally chip one five yards. And then chip one ten yards. And then 20 and up and up and up. Just exercises so that you can find the bottom of the golf swing, where the club connects with the ball, like you've been doing it for years. And once you've had a few lessons, you can do all of that short stuff in your garden, or in a park, and then you can move onto a driving range.

And then it's just about getting yourself out there. Not too soon. You don't want to go out too early, swing and miss the ball a few times and get disheartened. But you don't want to stay on the range for too long either.

The pitch and putt courses are a great middle ground. Nice, short holes, 70 or 80 yards long so that you can get to the greens quickly. I grew up playing that sort of golf. It doesn't matter how many shots you take, it doesn't matter if you four putt the ball, you're on the course and you're learning to play.

The more you're out there, the more chance that you'll get those lovely shots where you know you've nailed it by the sound. And the more good shots you play, the more you sort of subconsciously develop. It feels so good, you want to do it again and again.

If you don't go on the course, you won't learn how to play. You'll get used to hitting off a tee or a flat mat. Once you're on a golf course, you've got different lies, you're hitting balls on slopes or in grass or in rough. You've got bunkers and water. You're being tested. But in those early stages, wait for your confidence to build up. Go from the range to the pitch and putt. Go off the junior tees which can often be a hundred or so yards closer to the hole. Every time you hit a ball, you learn a little bit more about the game and about yourself. Even when it's going wrong. And it *will* go wrong.

My coach always has a saying for this. If you mess up, if you hook a ball into the pond or lift your wedge shot right over the green and onto the clubhouse roof, he always says the same thing.

'Just do a better job of it next time.'

I think that's the secret. You just keep doing the right thing, nudging yourself along. Don't overthink it. Once you get to a certain level, it's basically all mental. It really is. It's all mental. Your brain will keep trying to talk you out of doing something and you just have to keep telling it to fuck off.

If you miss one shot, you can go into full-blown panic stations. It can be a shot that you've played a thousand times, a simple chip onto the green or a drive off the tee, and all of a sudden you're overthinking it and getting it wrong. I've certainly been guilty of that in the past.

This is a sport where there's a really long time to think about stuff. You're going on a long walk, you've got time for your brain to talk to you about how badly you're doing. I had some time out of the game because that became a problem for me. But I also learned how to deal with it and how to cope with the pressure I was putting on myself. More on that later …

You have to remember how quickly things can change in golf. There's a reason why professional players don't give up on a tournament just because they've had a bad first day. There's always the possibility that something incredible can happen.

I remember back in 2011 when I'd qualified to play in The Open for the first time. I'd had to go into a play-off and the process went on so long that the sun went down and we had to go away and regroup in the morning. I won it on the 2nd hole and I was over the moon, but I just wanted to play more golf.

A couple of weeks later, my brother James decided to dust off his old clubs and play a round with me.

He might be the angriest golfer ever. We played a charity day, him, me and my sister, and it was Stableford rules, so there were points for every hole. It was just a bit of fun, but he was on the green and missed a putt, and he lost it and just smacked the ball straight off the green. 'What are you doing?' I said. 'You can still win points here.' He whipped around and shouted, 'Oh fuck the points!' But he hasn't played in ages and he is horrible out there. The sort of golf that is so bad it's difficult to watch because you don't know what to say. The sixth hole at my club is near the clubhouse, so he wants to give up and go in. I convinced him to stick it out, but he wasn't getting any better. The seventh and eighth hole are just as bad and by the time he gets to the ninth, he's basically given up.

He tosses the ball down and steps up to hit it and I'm looking at him, thinking, 'That's a terrible lie, he can't hit it from there!'

But he does hit it. He takes his eight iron and he lets rip with the best shot he's played all day, the best shot he's probably played in his life. He hits it flush, it goes straight towards the flag, one bounce, two bounce and it's in the hole. I was laughing so much I couldn't even stand up. A hole in one. And he was about to walk off the course.

It's an incredible sport and it's all the more incredible

when you remember that you can still play golf in your old age. This isn't a sport where someone can slide tackle you from behind and break your leg. You've got the rest of your life to improve. Golf is always teaching you stuff about yourself. You're always learning. Golf is like managing yourself. It's managing your emotions and your attitude. And those are skills that you can take into anything else in life. Absolutely anything.

So yeah, it's about hitting the ball, it's about being with people, it's about challenging yourself, it's about winning competitions. But mostly it's about those beautiful mornings. I promise you, there's nothing like it.

2

FROM AMATEUR TO PROFESSIONAL

If you're an amateur footballer, you turn professional when a scout spots you and their football club signs you up. If you're an amateur musician, it might happen when an A&R man turns up at your gig and signs you to a music label. In golf, it's all a bit different.

You're a professional from the first time you play for proper prize money. That's it. And from that moment on, you're basically self-employed. You're your own boss and all you need to do to stay in a job is to get out there, hit golf balls and do well in competitions. So no pressure, right?

It's the best life in the world. You travel, you play golf, you have a laugh. And yet the funny thing is that there was a point when I didn't want to be a professional at all. I didn't even want to pick up a golf club. The journey from amateur to professional isn't always smooth. But I'm getting ahead of myself.

I was about 14 when I first started to realise that I might be all right at this game. I'd grown quickly at school and I'm pretty much the same size now that I was back then, just a bit fatter. Because I had that physical strength, even at that age, it wasn't long before I was playing and beating adults.

When I was 15, I could hit the greens with my tee shot on some of the shorter par four courses at my local club. That's about 270 yards. That got the attention of a few people. Then I started to win competitions. Me and my dad won a foursomes tournament together. That was the best win of my career because I won it with my dad. I hit the winning putt and it was the same pressure I felt in Spain all those years later. The nerves don't really ever change.

I was winning scratch tournaments. You probably know this already, but just in case you're new to the sport, there's a handicap system in golf. It's what I was talking about in the last chapter; it's the system that allows me and anyone who can hit a ball to play together and still make the game interesting.

If we're playing a 72-hole golf course and you've got a handicap of ten and I don't have one at all then I need to go through all 18 holes in 72 shots to make par. If you do it in 81 shots, *you'll win* because your ten-shot handicap means that you will have finished one under par. Simple, right? It's one of the best things about golf.

The trouble is that they've changed how they work it out now. They've changed it to the point that even I don't understand it. But I don't need to understand it, to be fair, because I've been a professional since 2009 and we don't have handicaps.

Anyway, your average golf course usually only has a small percentage of people who have no handicap and I was one of them.

The secretary of Middlesex, Andy Williams, put me forward for an England training camp and it was almost like a trial. I went to Oxfordshire a few times, played a bit and then the following year I got selected for the proper England boys team. You play with a lot of kids when you're coming up through the ranks, but there's not many of you by this stage. You know you're in a really small percentage of golfers. And it was only then when I started thinking, 'I might be pretty good at this, you know?'

It was a great group too. Tommy Fleetwood, Eddie Pepperell, Matt Nixon, Matt Haines. There were loads of us. We had this coach giving us a session once and he was talking about the low odds of any of us making it on a professional tour. He looked at our group and said that he reckoned only one of us would be good enough to make the grade. Out of the ten of us there that day, literally seven of us got tour cards. How fucking wrong was that dude?

I absolutely loved it in that group, but I really struggled with the structure. I don't like following the crowd and I don't like being told what to do. I had a couple of running disagreements with some of the England coaches because I just wanted to do what I wanted to do.

The team we had that time, we had such a laugh. Honestly, it was so much fun. But once I moved into the men's squads, the proper England squads, it was a lot more serious. Like, way more serious. I hated it.

In the under-18s, we'd mess around all the time. We'd play golf wherever, we'd play pranks on each other and just have a good time. We were in a tournament in Canada once and we got to go on this boat trip down the rapids. We all got absolutely soaked and then afterwards someone decided to take their T-shirt off, give it the towel spin and then start whipping people. It escalated really quickly, it turned into a proper melee.

You might think with my build that I'd have been dominant, but I was just the chubby kid and I'm a big softie really. I've never been one to get into a fight, I don't even like having arguments. If you push me into a corner, I'll fight back, but I've gone my whole life without getting into fights and I'm not very good at them. When it all got broken up by the coaches and we all got bollocked, I think we were actually secretly relieved. I know I was.

Obviously, I was always the one getting caught with stuff like this. We were kicking medicine balls about in the gym once and I was the one who kicked it too hard and took out the ceiling tiles. That was a bad one.

We could have had a really bad one out with the Middlesex county players in Almería at a place called Desert Springs. Those boys were nuts and the whole trip was like a stag do. We found this bar out in the middle of nowhere one night. We got a cab out there, but we decided to walk back at 2 a.m. It was absolutely pitch black, no street lights and we all started messing around. There's nothing out there, nothing at all but a load of cactus and sure enough, someone decided to pick one up and chuck it into the group. It missed, but someone retaliated and tossed one in the other direction. And then we heard this massive fucking scream.

No word of a lie, this bloke has chucked a cactus full pelt into the darkness and it's hit one of the junior players right in the nipple. He was screaming his head off and I'm not even a bit surprised. I played with him in a tournament later that year and he was still pulling bits of cactus out of his tit four months later. It makes me feel sick to think about it now. What if it had hit him in the eye? The county days were crazy.

But the worst one for me was when we were up in Inverness for the home internationals. We were at this golf course called the Moray Golf Club and I'd had a really good week. I was winning game after game and so a few of us decided to go out and get absolutely hammered. We were all under 18 and so this was a very risky move.

We'd all get into trouble with the team manager if we got caught, but we figured we deserved to go out and have some fun.

I remember waking up in the Airbnb later that night and I was so hot. The window barely opened and so I pulled on a pair of shorts and a T-shirt and I went and stood outside. Now this is Inverness in the height of summer, so obviously it's fucking freezing and after a few minutes it starts to rain. I turned around to go back inside and discovered I'd locked myself out.

The rain was absolutely smashing down now and all of a sudden I was no longer too hot. I knew that I couldn't risk ringing the bell because I was still pissed and I'd get in trouble, so I made a run for the golf club itself. I tried all the doors and then found one at the back that was unlocked. I slipped inside and lay down in the locker room, soaking wet, and went to sleep again. Everything would have been fine if I'd stayed asleep – I could have slipped back and pretended I'd been for an early walk. But I got the thirst again and went on the hunt for some water. The first door I opened went into the main clubhouse and that's when all the lights came on and the alarms went off. The next thing I knew there were blue lights flashing outside the front door. I'd had better nights.

I didn't know what the fuck I was going to do, I was panicking, thinking I was about to get arrested. I waved the police officers down and explained what had happened and you know what? They were really cool about it. They asked where I was staying and they took me back, but of course the door was still locked.

So this police officer picked a window and started throwing stones at it to wake someone up. And whose window did he pick? The team manager's. So this geezer pulled back the curtain, looked down all confused and saw two police officers and me looking sorry for myself. I still remember his face even now. He looked like he wanted to kill me. That really didn't go down well.

They pulled me in for all of these meetings, they wanted to know who I'd been out with, but I'm not a grass. I just kept telling them that I'd been on my own, that I just wanted a couple of pints, but I think that made it worse. They must have thought I had a drinking problem. They kept pushing, but I didn't sell anyone out.

I got banned for the following year's winter training and missed out on a trip to Holland. But it was funny, so what can you do?

That was the boy's team. Just a constant laugh. The men's team wasn't like that at all.

Everything was monitored, everything was written down. There were drills and schedules and we even had to write stuff. Fucking hell, I just wanted to play golf. I was, like, what? Why are we sitting here writing shit when I could be out there hitting putts? Just fuck off and leave me alone.

Some people could handle it. Some people were happy to follow instructions and do what they were told, but it wasn't for me. We were doing these pitching drills one day, but I knew that I was driving the ball really bad at the time and I was annoyed about it, so I just teed up a driver and started smacking balls around, which was kind of funny, but I got a telling off for it.

I remember this one argument. We were having a two-day competition in the group and the fitness trainer wanted us to do a nine-hole run. That's about three miles. The day before the competition! I thought he was fucking mental. I was like, 'Why would I go running on the evening before a competition?'

He was saying, 'You gotta do it,' and I was like, 'I fucking don't, mate.' I got really fed up with stuff like that.

It wasn't all the coaches, don't get me wrong. There were some great guys there like Alan Thompson and Graham Walker, they understood me. If I had an issue or got into a bit of trouble, one of them would pull me to one side.

But I couldn't get my head around it. I just wanted to do my own thing and my golf … well, it got a lot worse really quickly. I stopped getting selected. And then my dad passed away and I just went right off the whole thing. I didn't even pick up a club for six months. That's how I ended up on that building site dragging those fire doors off the back of a lorry.

It was all too serious. Me and my dad had played a lot together and that was fun. And then it was fun in the boys' teams with all of my mates. And then it just got too much. I didn't think I had much of a chance of turning professional at that point, so I drifted. I didn't want to play, I didn't want to go into a tournament. I was just, 'Nah, you're all right.'

And it was John, one of the guys from the club who changed it. He wandered past the building site one day. He was a member up at the club, and he pulled me to one side and said, 'What are you doing here? You should be on the golf course. Go up and play, I'll set you up with a game against my mate, go on, get back out there.'

I was like, 'Fuck, no!' but he kept on and on at me and finally coaxed me back. It had been six months since I'd picked up a club, but I just turned up and flushed it. Eighteen holes. Absolutely smashed it. I didn't realise at the time, but the guys were all looking out for me, trying to get me back in the game. I'd probably still be on the building site if they hadn't got involved.

So I finished that round and the guy I was playing, Shaun Reddin, said, 'Why don't you get back into competitions?'

But I didn't want to get back into the amateur stuff, I was done with that.

So he said, 'Well, why don't you turn pro?'

Now you probably know this already, but if you're new to the sport, you should know that it's not quite like football where you have lots of divisions and promotion and relegation. But it might help you to think of it like that for now.

Let's leave LIV Golf out of the conversation for now because at the time I'm writing this book, no-one's got a fucking clue how that's going to work. You've got your PGA Tour, which is the biggest tour of all. If you do really well and get a PGA Tour card, it means you've got a year playing in tournaments all over the world and the prize money is massive. Like, millions of dollars for competitions.

You've got the European Tour, which is really big too. But again, you've got to get your tour card before they let you on. And it's not easy.

Underneath that you've got the Challenge Tour, which is a feeder for the European Tour. Under the Challenge Tour is the EuroTour. Still with me?

Usually the best young players turn pro quickly because they're spotted in the best amateur competitions, like the Walker Cup, and they get picked up by managers who will get them a few starts on the Challenge Tour. Sometimes they might even get them a few starts on the European Tour itself. But I wasn't moving in those circles anymore.

But then there's this thing below all of them called the Jamega Tour, it's a developmental tour in the UK. You pay your entry money, you play for prize money and that's it. You're a pro! You literally don't even need to sign anything. You just play your first event and that's all.

Shaun said he'd help me out financially. He said, 'Look, just give it a go. Give it a year or so and see how you get on. If you don't do well then at least you've tried.'

So I gave it a go. I played a few Jamegas and ended up winning one. Then I went to European Tour qualifying school, a three-stage event. I got through the first stage, I didn't make it to the end, but it gave me a bit of confidence, which I really needed back then. I played a few more Jamegas and did well enough to get on that EuroTour.

And then the breakthrough came. I was at an event at the Burhill Golf Club and I knew I was first reserve for a Challenge Tour event in Austria. Remember, that's the one just below the big European Tour. If one person drops out, then I'm in. I'm playing for decent money. It's a massive, massive opportunity.

Now I know I said some things about mobile phones on the golf course earlier, but give me a break. I'm playing this competition and I am literally checking my phone every 20 minutes. Come on, come on, come on. And then bang. There it is. I get a text message telling me that I'm in.

I had to finish the round, pull out of the tournament, get myself home and start packing. I was flying to Austria the next day. I didn't even get there in time to have a look at the course. The first time I saw it was when I teed off on it the next morning. I ended up finishing third and winning myself £12,000 in the process.

It was crazy. Absolutely crazy. But it wasn't about the money. I didn't really even think about that bit. All I cared about was that the third-place finish got me into a tournament the following week in France. And I did well there too, I made the cut. All of a sudden I was 40th in the rankings for that year. Suddenly I'm shooting 16 under in four-day tournaments and I was like, 'Fucking hell! Do you know what? I can actually do this!' All my confidence came flooding back.

It was mad to think that this all happened barely three years after I'd put my clubs down and walked away from the sport. Three years since I'd been dragging around those fucking fire doors. Shaun became my manager shortly after that. He was there when I needed someone to believe in me, and while we're not working together now, I'll never forget what he did. I wouldn't be playing professionally now without him.

But here's the thing that most people don't realise about playing on a tour: you have to pay to put yourself through it. It's not like playing for Arsenal, where you get on a plane chartered by the club and fly to a hotel booked by the club and play in kit supplied by the club. From start to finish in golf, you have to pay for everything yourself.

The entry fees go right down when it gets to this level, but it's the travel and accommodation that are the killer. In most cases, you've got to fly out for the competition. You'll need a hire car to get you from the airport to the hotel. Oh, and you need a hotel. Now sometimes it all lines up and you get a really good deal, but sometimes it's so expensive that you literally can't afford to go.

And even if you can go, you know that you have to play well just to break even. It gets crazy expensive really quickly.

If it costs you two or three grand just to play in a tournament and you don't get anything if you fail to make the cut, imagine how you feel as you're going around the course. Imagine how that pressure builds.

So, of course, you have to look for bargains. Forget about your chartered jets, it's all Ryanair and easyJet. And you don't want any of those extra costs. I had one flight where my bag was overweight and they wouldn't let me on. The only thing I could do was just put all of my clothes on to get through security. So I'm walking through with four T-shirts and couple of jumpers, a pair of jeans with jogging bottoms over the top. I got some pretty funny looks, but got through security, bought myself a hand luggage bag and shoved the clothes all back in there. I was with my brother at the time, he was in bits, laughing his head off.

And there are certainly days when I'd rather be a darts player. They can put the tools of their trade in their pocket. I'm lugging 30 kilos of golf clubs everywhere and so there's always a weight issue. It's an absolute nightmare. And it doesn't matter who you fly with, they're all shit in my opinion.

I've had trips where I've miscounted things. This one time I played golf with my friends on a Sunday night. And it's one of those when you go out for one pint and it turns into ten. I've gone home and packed my suitcase before falling asleep and then hauling myself up for the early flight. I got to the hotel, opened the case and for some reason I've got ten pairs of trousers and only two shirts. I had to sit there in my hotel room trying to wash clothes in the sink and get them dry after a full day on the course.

Another time I turned up and the only clothes I'd brought were a pair of purple trousers and a purple shirt. I was like, 'I can't wear this, man. I can't do this.'

And my mate, who was caddying for me, said, 'You've just gotta do it. Just get out there and rock it.'

Easier said than done. I turned up at the club all in purple and the first person who saw me said, 'Hello Barney!' I was like, 'Fuck's sake, this is going to be a long day.'

But I loved that life. I absolutely loved it. I went to Kazakhstan and did well, I went to Russia and finished second. I played in seven or eight events and I wasn't embarrassing myself in any of them. In fact, I was doing pretty well. And all of that put me into the final event of the season in a really good position. You see, the top 15 of the Challenge Tour win themselves a European Tour card and that's the ticket to the big time.

That final event was in Italy and Shaun set it all up. The hotel on the San Domenico Resort was £300 a night so there was no fucking chance we were staying there. We could never stay at places like that, it was always tiny hotels or weird little places on Airbnb.

Though they rarely came as weird as this.

So Shaun books this place on Airbnb. There was him, me, my girlfriend at the time, my caddie and my brother, and I don't know how he managed it, but Shaun has booked a one-bedroom place. One bedroom! This tiny little double bed and then these fucking bunk beds.

This is the night before a competition that could change my life and we walked in, saw the beds, and just started crying with laughter.

But there was nothing we could do, we just had to get on with it. And it was so bad that it became even funnier, we couldn't stop laughing about it all week. This was one of the most pressurised tournaments of my life and it didn't matter. There were five of us in one room. It was fucking hilarious.

I had a good first day, shot four under, but lots of people had good days too and the leaderboard was pretty bunched up. Another four under on the second day put me in eighth position, six shots back from Tommy Fleetwood, who was out in front, and we ended up in the same group for the final day.

I've never found that it matters too much who you're playing with in a tournament. You've got to concentrate on what you're doing, not what someone else is up to. And I really needed to concentrate for this one because it was so windy. But it was strange. I didn't feel the pressure as much as you'd think. For me, a place on the European Tour was way beyond my expectations. I was just happy to be on the Challenge Tour. If you'd offered me that at the start of the season, I'd have bitten your hand off. But as we worked our way around the course, I realised that I might not be playing Challenge Tour golf next season after all.

On that final hole, I was just off to the right from the green, about 25 yards away from the flag. I pulled out a wedge and played a nice little chip and run onto the green where it came to rest just two feet from the hole.

There were leaderboards everywhere, so I knew the situation. I knew that if I put it down, I'd finish third in the tournament and 15th on the tour, and that would be the European Tour card. And now I'm shitting my pants.

Because this is the problem with golf. You can miss from two feet. People do it all the time. I've done it. I still do it every now and then. You shouldn't. The percentages are really low. But it happens. And I can't even just step up and get it down because everyone else has to take their shot first. All I can do is mark it, put the ball in my pocket and step away.

The wait can be awful and it can really play on your mind. I usually take a look, assess the surface, see if I can work out which way it's going to break, and then I walk away and try to take my mind somewhere else. I might think about Arsenal's next game, I might think about what I'm going to have for dinner. Sometimes I'll run through our Christmas plans or think about what I can barbecue when I get home. Anything to get the mind going in a different direction. And then it's time.

Two feet. You step up and you have to make your decision. You have to know what you're going to do and how you're going to hit it, and then you have to stick to it. Two feet. Pick your line. Two feet. Make the decision. Two feet.

You hear it off the face of the putter. You know the noise. You always know. And then there's a different noise, that soft plop as it drops into the hole. The sweetest noise you've ever heard. And in that moment is a sense of relief like nothing you've ever felt before.

And then all I could think was, 'Is it really enough?'

I knew I'd finished third, but I was tied with someone else. Did it still count? Was it still really enough? I went to sign my scorecard and I've never spent so much time over it. You can get a one-shot penalty if you fill it in incorrectly and that would destroy everything. Is it really enough?

It *was* enough. Confirmation came in that I had secured 15th and that I was going on the European Tour. Holy shit. That is insane. I was like, 'What the fuck?!'

I was going on the European Tour to some of the greatest golf courses in the world, playing with some of the greatest golfers in the world, genuine household names. And that's what excited me. Obviously the money was huge, but that wasn't why I was celebrating. It was the thought of hitting the big time.

I never saw it coming. It felt like it happened overnight. I played seven or eight Challenge Tour events and the next thing I know I'm looking at the European Tour. Everything became real. And it really didn't sink in because it happened so fast.

But it wasn't an entirely successful week. The thing with these tournaments is that you play Wednesday to Saturday and then there's a pro-am on the Sunday where you play a round with amateur players. But I've just won my European Tour card, so we chuck this party on Saturday night and I get absolutely smashed.

The morning after, my caddy is shaking me and shouting, 'Mate! We're teeing off in less than an hour,' and I'm just like, 'Oh no.'

I was still hammered. I'd been out until 4 a.m., I think I was still drunk. And I remember getting to the golf course and thinking, 'Oh, fuck me.'

I played a few holes and the hangover started to kick in. But the guys I was playing with had a load of beers. One of them cracked one open and said, 'Do you want one?'

'Absolutely!' I said. So I had three or four while we were going round. But little did I know that you're not allowed to drink on a Pro-Am and so I got fined £500. I couldn't give a shit, to be honest. That party was mad.

It was a great time. And it was only the start of my life as a professional golfer. A life where you get to be your own boss.

You've got no-one there to tell you what to do, there's no team to represent. You're out there on your own, for yourself. Like I said earlier, it's like being self-employed, It's all up to you how you want to do it. That suited me. That suited me a lot more. If I fuck up, that's fine. It's on me. Some people struggle with that, they need structure, but I just love floating around doing my own thing.

I went back to North Mid that Christmas and we had a massive party. I remember thinking, I'll take it easy tonight because I'm a European Tour player now. I'll just have the one pint. That went well. Next thing I know I've gone out onto the course pissed and lost all of the expensive water-proof clothes I've been sent by my sponsors.

Eight weeks later I was out in South Africa for the first event of the season and, deep down, I was just starting to feel like I might be out of my comfort zone.

3

TEEING OFF

It's impossible to talk about teeing off without instantly thinking about *Happy Gilmore*, isn't it? I must have watched that movie two hundred times and it's just one of the all-time great golf films. But Adam Sandler's famous shot, where he runs up to the tee and spanks it, is really, really HARD to do.

I've had mixed outcomes with that shot. I've sent a couple straight, but I nearly killed someone with it on the 10th at North Mid. That tee is right next to the 11th green, it's just ten yards off to the right, so anyone putting there is already in danger from a serious mis-hit. They certainly were this time.

I've run up, gone to swing it, slipped on the wet grass and I've smashed it out of the toe of the club. It's screamed across the green at waist height, right through a group of golfers and away into the distance. I'm lying on my arse, my mates are all howling with laughter at me and those poor blokes are just staring at us thinking, 'What the fuck just happened?'

If you are going to try it, and please try to be more careful than I was, then it's all about the footwork. The two sidesteps are key. You've got to get your measurements right. I was too far away, I was reaching to get the ball and that's why I stacked it. All I can say is that Adam Sandler deserves all the credit he gets for that movie.

Padraig Harrington actually went through a stage of teeing off that like in competition. There's a great video of him at Valhalla in 2014 on YouTube – he doesn't let on that he's about to do it and you can hear the crowd laughing in surprise when he lets it rip. But that's Padraig, he's always thinking outside the box, trying to get ahead of everyone.

There's logic in it. It's all about the force of the connection, isn't it? You've got to think about the swing like an elastic band. You want to let go at the maximum, you want it to be tight at the top. You're loading all that weight on your right side (if you're right-handed) and then letting go. If you've got the momentum of moving forward as well, it's like running up and throwing a punch as opposed to standing still and throwing one.

Unfortunately, what you might gain in power, you'll lose on control and so, as I proved, you really only increase your chances of braining a middle-aged man trying to putt for birdie on the 11th.

But it's hardly surprising that Sandler chose to make a movie about someone who was really good at teeing off, as opposed to someone who was really good at getting out of sand traps. Teeing off is an incredible moment, there's very little like it in any other sport. There's just something very basic and very amazing about watching someone hit a ball really, really hard.

Whether you're an amateur playing at your local golf course or a professional on the 1st hole of a Major, teeing off is the ultimate test of nerve because there's so much that can go wrong. Golf can be so cruel and brutal – a disaster can happen at any time. One bad tee shot can lead to a triple bogey and then, if you're not out of contention, you're going to have to do very well to get back in.

You can hit balls on the range before the day starts, you can practise, but when you step out for your first drive, it's something else. It's probably the longest shot you'll play, it's the only shot that you can tee up and it's the one with the smallest margin for error. If you're even slightly out with it then it's going to go a long way off line, unlike a pitching wedge, say, which doesn't do anywhere near the distance.

When I tee it up on an opening hole, I'm always nervous. That first shot, that first swing. You just want to get it right so that you can settle in to your round. And when you're at a big tournament, like a Major, it's even more difficult. They build up the stands around the tee box and sometimes it can feel really claustrophobic. That's when the heart rate starts to accelerate. And sometimes you're facing an absolute bastard of a hole too.

I remember playing the 2019 Open at the Dunluce Links at Royal Portrush, and that was a brutal first tee. It was all out of bounds to the left and guess which way the wind was blowing? Right to left and really hard too. That was awful. I even went at it with a two iron to try to minimise the risk, but you could see it turning on the wind and I was lucky to get away with it. A lot of people didn't that day. It gets into your head, it plays on your mind. You can hear your brain going, 'Don't let it go left, don't let it go left, don't shut the face and hit it left,' and then you know exactly what's going to happen.

I've spoken to lots of footballers about golf and the only way I can describe it is that it's like taking a penalty kick in a big tournament. You've got time to think, you've got ALL the time to think.

Some people have little quirks or superstitions, they shuffle their feet or wiggle their arses, or they have to use a certain colour tee, but I haven't got anything like that.

One of the worst things in golf is when you're asked to play a provisional ball. This happens if you hit a shot so wild that no-one's even sure if you'll be able to find it. So you have to hit a back-up option so the whole tournament doesn't grind to a halt while you're on your hands and knees in the woods trying to find your ball. It's really awful. The announcer will tell the crowd what's happening and this terrible hush falls because everyone is thinking, 'Hur, hur, no pressure, mate.' And then you have to try not to fuck that shot up as well.

I remember one tournament on the Challenge Tour where the event was held up by about 15 minutes because people were losing their balls off the first tee so often. It was horrible, you've got a great big logjam of golfers standing around watching their mates taking two or three attempts just to get moving because they keep smashing it out of bounds. By the time it's your turn, you're no longer bothered by how far you can hit it, you're just praying to get it somewhere on the fairway.

What I've learned through experience and through work with sports psychologists is that you've just got to go into your little bubble, get into your process. You tee the ball up, you take a practice swing, you concentrate on where you're going to hit in, what shot you're going to hit and then … you just stand up and hit it.

For me, you've got to hit it hard. Let it go. Hit it hard. Don't get caught in the middle, don't be negative. You've just got to stand up, hit it and then let it be. If you drop yourself into that process, if you have a really clear mind, a really clear idea of what sort of shot you're going to hit, you find that you forget everything else that's going on around you. In some sense, I think the trick is to trick your brain. Because if you don't, you can really get yourself in a bad place.

There's one hole in Abu Dhabi, it's a par three, and there's a big expanse of water in front of the green. On the weekend, they put the pin right at the front, so you've got a choice. You can be aggressive, take the hole on and chase the birdie. Or you can take the water out of the equation, aim for the middle of the green, ten yards further than the pin, but definitely on the green. You might hole a long one for birdie, or you might just give yourself an easy finish.

It's do-able. It's not a great distance, just an eight iron to get in there. But it's tricky to suss out the wind, and that can make all the difference. So up I step and hit the ball.

There are certain signs you get when you've messed up. Sometimes you can feel it in the strike, sometimes there's a bad noise. And then you know. But sometimes there's no sign, you haven't done anything wrong, you've just got caught by the wind. If the wind is coming back to you, it'll make the ball balloon up in the air and you see it. You're looking up thinking it's a bit higher than usual and then you realise. And then you hear that wet plop as the ball vanishes forever.

There's nothing like that feeling. You hit a shot over water and you're watching it, thinking, 'Go on, go on, go on,' and then as it comes down you're either thinking, 'Sit, sit, sit' or 'Oh fuck!'

So you take out another ball and you have another go. And you do the same thing again. Plop. And now you're on your third ball and you've got peanut butter mouth and you can't think straight and the crowd are absolutely loving it. The bastards.

People are always sitting around those kind of par threes because they want the action. They want to see people making birdies, they want a hole in one, but they also want to see people making sevens and eights. All of the players know it.

They're thinking, 'Oh, is he going to fuck this up here? He's got a two-shot lead, he's seven under, what's he going to do? Is he going to hold his nerve or is he going to pieces?'

You try to regroup, you try not to take any notice, but you can hear that voice in your head going, 'Oh fucking hell, mate, what are you doing here?'

And you have to say it in your head, because you can get some pretty heavy fines for bad language. I've been very lucky in the past because I've got a bit of a potty mouth. Either the microphone hasn't been close enough or it hasn't been live, but there's been a few times when I've hit a shot and screamed, 'You fucking twat!' but somehow I've never been told off for it.

Sometimes it's not your voice that you have to worry about, it's the spectators' voices. On some golf courses, especially the links, people don't realise how their voice travels on the wind. They think they're being quiet, but you can hear everything they're saying. And that can really piss people off. But that's not really their fault. Sometimes, though, people are just arseholes.

This one time I was about to tee off and some guy's phone went off. So I stopped my swing and turned to look at him, but he didn't put it down. He just took a couple of backwards steps and then he took the call! I'm not usually confrontational, I try to leave it to my caddy to be bad cop, but that's one of the times where I was just like, 'Mate! Get off your fucking phone!' and he just gave me this gesture as if to say, 'Hang on a minute, I'm on the phone here,' and that made all the spectators start shouting at him until he gave up and ended the call. Who even has their phone switched on while they're watching golf? Mad.

Some players really get affected by stuff like this. One of the funniest things I've seen on the tee box is those marshals with the 'quiet' signs. Some players just get really thrown by them if they stand a bit too close or they move a bit too late. I've seen players turn around and have a go at them, telling them to go away. It's just nerves. Some golfers, their hearing is amazing, they can pick up anything. I don't understand it, but it is funny to watch. It's best not to take any chances if you're at the golf, just get to where the players can't see you and you'll never get in an argument with them.

Everyone gets nerves. It's such a strange thing. Put any amateur on the first tee and get ten people to watch them and you'll see them go to pieces. They're a nervous wreck. I've seen it so many times where people rush their tee shot because they can hear the next group coming up behind them and they're scared of playing a bad shot in front of people. People absolutely hate it.

It fades a bit with experience. It's all about understanding yourself and learning how to manage it. I've done other sports, crossover stuff, and I've been way more nervous about throwing a dart in front of a darts player or kicking a ball in front of a footballer because I'm out of my comfort zone. But I've hit thousands of tee shots and I've hit so many bad ones in my time that I've become almost immune to it in some sense.

The nerves don't change, but you do. You start to

understand them, you know that they're coming and you know what they are. So you're not caught off guard. You can handle it.

But I've never felt nerves like those I had before teeing off at the 2011 Open. I'd only just started playing on the Challenge Tour at the time, hitting balls in front of a handful of people. I was still a few months away from that big finish and my first European Tour card. And then I went straight into a Major.

For weeks, I thought I was going to fall down the stairs and break something and then I wouldn't be able to play. I thought it might be my only Major ever. I was properly freaking out. And then I got there and it was even worse! I was there for three days of practice and all the players I've grown up watching are there, Phil Mickelson is there, Sergio García is there.

I was in the last group to go round, teeing off at 4 p.m., and so all the spectators have been out all day and they're all rowdy. I was bricking it. Absolutely bricking it. It was all a blur. And so I just stepped up, gave it a big swing and … it went just fine! Ended up on the fairway. But I didn't stop bricking it for the whole day.

The Open can be so punishing, especially when the weather is against you. I was working for Sky Sports for the 2023 Open at Royal Liverpool, which was the weekend when the rain wrecked England's chances of regaining the Ashes down the road at Old Trafford. Of course with golf, you don't stop for rain unless it's really, really bad. The only thing you'll definitely stop for is lightning, but that's more of a problem in the USA than it is in the UK.

So out they went into the downpour. There were so many tee shots that weekend, good connections, good power, but they rose up into the wind and then off they went, drifting off the fairway into the rough.

I've played in some awful weather. I've been sat in the clubhouse at the Dunhill Links watching the rain smash itself against the glass thinking, 'There's no way we're going out in this.' I've been off for a cup of tea and a sandwich and then someone's said, 'We're going out!' And I'm thinking, 'What?! Why?' In that sort of weather, sometimes I'll tee off with an iron just to make sure the ball doesn't vanish off somewhere.

The crosswind is a killer. You can't stop the wind from moving the ball when it really picks up, so you have to angle into it. But you can adjust your tee as well. The higher the tee sits in the turf, the more elevation you'll get, so you push it right down and then adjust your swing to make sure you punch it away at about head height.

It's tricky, but if you put the ball further back in your stance, aim a little further left and then get your hands in front of the club head so that you're changing the loft, that keeps everything low. You want to hit it flat and a bit softer. You see, the harder you hit the ball, the more the ball spins. And that's what makes it go up in the air. So you want to take all of that spin off it. You lose distance, but you've got more chance of staying on the fairway.

I'm all right for distance, I can get it out there a fair

way. But some of the players nowadays, this new generation, they're really training for length. This wasn't really a thing until Tiger Woods came along. When people saw how far he could hit it, everything changed.

We didn't practise to hit it long when I was a kid, but that's a huge part of the training now. People work on the speed of their swing, and they can hit it so far it's insane. If I'm swinging well, if I really force it, I can get a swing speed of about 120 mph. But you watch some of the guys now and they'll be up at 135 mph or even 140 mph. My ball speed will be 175 mph, but they're doing 190 mph and more.

And it's all in the training. It's all about the way you swing it. Unless you're prepared to break down your swing and start again, how you played as a kid determines how you play as an adult. So now they're turning a different way, using that force as they shift from the right to left. And they're just bombing it now.

Back in 1980, the top average-length driver on the PGA Tour was Dan Pohl with 274 yards. Forty years later it was Cameron Champ with 321 yards. And that was just his *average*.

The equipment has changed a bit too. I would have loved to have seen John Daly play with today's kit. He was hitting 300 yards back in the 1990s. He's in his mid-fifties now and he still hits it a long way. I've been lucky enough to play with him a bit and hang out, he's great. I thought I had a problem with authority, but he's way worse than me. If the rules are to wear a jacket and a tie then I'll probably moan for a bit and then give up. He won't. There's no chance he'd ever give in. He'd just turn up in whatever he wanted to wear. Legend.

The best tee shot I've ever seen was Darren Clarke in 2006 at the Ryder Cup. Incredible. His wife had died just a few months earlier and this was his first game back. He walks out and the crowd are going crazy, Americans and Europeans, all cheering for him. It must have been so tough to step up there, and that energy can sometimes have the reverse effect, fill him with too much adrenaline, but he steps up and just nails it, big hit, straight as an arrow. Unbelievable.

Tiger Woods was one of the best strikers of a ball of all time, if not the best. Just YouTube some of his career highlights. Watching him growing up was amazing. He was the first one to bring that power to the course. Ernie Els was another one – the way he swung it was incredible. Hence the nickname, the Big Easy. Vijay Singh was a big, tall dude, a real big hitter. But Tiger was something else. You'll never see a golfer with a stronger mental side of the game. He just seemed immune to pressure. I think it all came from his dad and the way he was almost military trained to be the best in the world.

When I grew up, I'd go to the golf club with my mates, steal a buggy out of the shed, play some holes and there'd be six of us hanging off the buggy, slamming it around, hitting balls at each other and messing around. I don't think Tiger's upbringing was quite like that …

4

THE EUROPEAN TOUR

Going out on the European Tour for the first time was like my first day at school all over again. New people, new places, new rules to try to follow.

I don't know that I prepared particularly well. As I said earlier, I tried to keep a low profile that Christmas, but I fucked that up by getting battered on Christmas Eve in the Wetherspoons in North Finchley and losing all my new sponsored kit. It all came around so quickly.

The first event was out in South Africa in January 2012 and I had no idea what to expect. It had been such a whirlwind. One minute I was on the building site, not even thinking about golf, then I was on a Jamega event, and before I knew it I'd played fewer than a dozen Challenge Tour events and then it was like, 'Oh shit, I'm on the European Tour!'

It was all quite low key at first. There weren't too many of the big names out that early, but I saw a few familiar faces. Tommy Fleetwood was out there, it was good to see him again. It was a whole new level for me and I found it challenging at first. I missed the cut by a bit, then went to Johannesburg and missed the cut by a lot. I went round in 68 on the first day and then shit my pants and posted 78 on the second day. And that was it for a couple of months.

When you squeeze onto the tour like I did, your ranking isn't high enough to get you through the front door of some of the really prestigious events. I didn't get to play in the big money events in the Middle East or India and it wasn't until March that I got a chance to play again, this time in Spain. And this time I made the cut, earning myself £1,800 for four days in Andalucía and a 70th-place finish.

That, by the way, is one of the weirdest things about being a professional golfer. Everyone can go onto the internet and find out exactly what you've earned from one tournament to the next. I've got used to it over the years, but it's so odd. I'd always get a few comments whenever I went home if I'd played well. 'Nice bit of a cash for a few days' work, Beef,' and that sort of thing. Of course, what people don't realise is that you have to pay for everything along the way. You've got your travel, your hotel, your caddie, management fees. And if you don't make the cut, you don't get a penny. It's sort of like high-stakes sports betting, except you're always betting on yourself, whacking down a couple of grand every time a tournament comes up.

That was a big moment, making that cut. I made it on my very last shot, holing a 40-foot putt to scrape over the line. It was such a relief because I was beginning to have some doubts about myself. I don't think I ever expected to retain my card that year. It was always going to be hard when you're not allowed to play in the tournaments with the most points on offer. You miss out on those and you're fucking miles behind in the rankings right from the start, playing catch-up for the rest of the season. No, I saw it as good experience, a chance to really test myself and improve my game.

But while I missed a lot of cuts in 2012, I was never missing by very much, it was always just a handful of shots. I was close. And I was just happy to be there. I kept thinking, 'How the fuck have I got a European Tour card?' In my wildest dreams, I'd never expected anything like that. I was just happy to be travelling around the world and playing the game that I loved. It was very different to the way I'd feel about golf just five years later.

Financially, it was okay. I started to improve and I posted a couple of top 50 finishes, and the prize money from there, just under ten grand each time, along with a couple of modest sponsorship deals, kept me in good shape. I could afford to get myself around the world and play, but it was obvious that I was heading back down to the Challenge Tour for 2013.

But again, I wasn't bothered. I'd heard people say that it was a really difficult tour to get out of, that you could be stuck down there for years, but I didn't see it. I'd got out of it almost instantly in 2011, so I backed myself to do it again. My mindset was perfect: I was there for the experience, I'd gained that experience and I'd be back in a year's time.

And then I got injured.

I was playing with a mate on Royal St George's and after about eight holes I started to get a pain in my shoulder. I didn't like that one bit. I struggled to finish the round and it was getting really uncomfortable. I thought it would sort itself out over Christmas, but when I came back for the first Challenge Tour it wasn't right at all. It turned out to be something called bursitis and it took nearly six months to sort it out. By the time I was playing again, it wasn't a question of doing well enough to get back on the European Tour. I was desperately trying to rack up enough points just to stay on the Challenge Tour.

That was a really stressful year. I was genuinely shitting myself that I might slip off the bottom and then it would have been a nightmare trying to claw my way back. You end up back in that world of playing mini-tours and hoping that someone calls in sick so that you can get an invite. I ended up surviving by the skin of my teeth. You had to finish in the top 80 to stay on, and I came 78th.

The next season was completely different. After all that stress and anxiety, I was fully fit, fully rested and ready to rock. I played some amazing golf right from the start, I won a couple of events and I ended the season at the top of the rankings by some distance, winning the Challenge Tour Order of Merit.

I was learning more too. I was getting myself in good situations, leading tournaments from the front, or getting in brilliant battles with the best golfers on that tour; those days where you're matching each other shot for shot and it's all about who blinks first. It was a good, consistent season and it got me back where I still didn't quite feel that I belonged: the European Tour.

I didn't feel the same way I did in 2012 by this stage. It was no longer enough just to be there for the experience. I didn't want to go back down to the Challenge Tour, I wanted to keep my card and start to really compete. And I couldn't have got off to a better start. I finished third in the Alfred Dunhill in South Africa and picked up my biggest cheque so far, just over £100,000. But the money wasn't anything compared with the way I felt now. I'd kept up the pace across all four days, I'd recovered from a wobbly start on the last day, played the back nine one under and birdied the 18th. Now I felt like I could hold my own at this level and the points gave me a really strong foundation for the season objective of keeping my tour card.

But the money was weird. I'd never really had any before. Up until now, it had gone in one side and come out the other, taken up with all the travel and expenses. But this was a serious chunk, especially as I was still living at home. It meant that I could get a few big rounds in at home, because where's the fun in just hoarding it? I wanted to make sure everyone had a good time. But it also meant I was set up for the season. I could focus on the golf without worrying about whether or not I could afford to get anywhere. And it helped. I only missed two cuts in the next eight tournaments.

It was steady progress, the sort of consistency I needed at that stage. I didn't get another big result until Scotland in the summer. I've always loved Scotland. The crowds are great, the coastline is beautiful, everyone is so friendly. Being in Scotland is good for the soul.

It was good for my rankings as well. I finished 17th and I was looking in decent shape for the season until a couple of poor performances left me in jeopardy again. Nothing's ever easy. It took a top ten finish in Turkey to make it certain that I'd still be playing on the tour in 2016. And that was where it all got really crazy.

I was feeling at home on the tour now. There were some good guys out there, the social scene was decent and I wasn't celebrating every time I made the cut, I was playing as if I expected to make it. I came 4th in Qatar, 15th in Perth, I made six of eight cuts and then I didn't play for six weeks ahead of the visit to Valderrama in Spain. And that course was a hard one. I played nine holes in the Pro-Am there before it started and I was shitting myself.

It was so tight off the first tee that it felt like you could get easily blocked out. The fairways were treacherous. If you didn't really think about where you were going, if you didn't plan in advance, you could wind up in all sorts of trouble. But the weather was perfect and I don't know if it was just because I was well rested, but I had a brilliant day out there, I was bogey free and one shot off the lead after the first day, just behind Alexander Levy. But he had a bad couple of days and fell away. He wasn't the only one. The wind arrived on day two and everyone struggled, only a couple of players got round under par and I was happy enough with a 74. When you have wind on a course where the greens are really firm and fast and you've got rough either side of the fairway that's like a jungle, it's not a matter of opening up a lead, it's a matter of not fucking up and just trying to stay with the chasing pack. The next day, it was more of the same and with another 74, I felt like I had a good finish in me.

Everyone was talking about the conditions in the locker room. There were some seriously good players out there. Sergio García was there, it was one of his favourite courses usually, but not this time. Martin Kaymer was up there, he was doing really well. But I didn't think too much about them, I was just trying to focus on myself.

On that final day, I was pretty nervous. The wind had died down but I wasn't playing anywhere near my best. I felt like something was wrong with my set-up and this was just about the worst time to reach that conclusion. I teed off at the fourth and it veered off to the left. As I walked towards it, I decided to try something different.

I stood up to the ball and I tried to alter my stance. I dropped my hips and made them sit a bit further backwards, nothing drastic, but just a bit of a change of angle. I figured that it was a lay-up shot, I was just trying to get it on the green. If I got it wrong, I probably wouldn't get it too far wrong.

I got it so right.

I hit that ball so flush and so sweet that it just ripped off through the air, exactly where I wanted it. I felt amazing.

I'd had a problem, I'd fixed the problem, I was in control. For the next few holes I was in the zone, absolutely buoyant. I was making difficult shots, putting myself in great places and the holes were falling away.

There's no feeling like it, the sense that everything was going my way. And then I bogied the 14th. That was nerves. That was all nerves. I went to the 15th and I glanced at the leaderboard.

I was at the top. I was at the top of the fucking leaderboard with four holes to go. My caddie, Gordon 'Gordy' Faulkner, was ice cool. 'Just give yourself four birdie putts here,' he said, 'and you'll have a chance.'

The 15th was a really difficult par three. I hit a good shot onto the green, just missed the putt for birdie, but I walked away thinking, 'That's okay. That's all right. Take the par and move on.'

I got the tee shot away on the 16th, dropped it onto the green with the second and then put it away with the third. Birdie. And that was when my brain started to go nuts. I tried to shrug it off and I walked down to the 17th, but I could feel my heart going and my hands sweating. I tried to focus on getting the tee shot away and not fucking it up. And away it went. Straight down the fairway. My brain was going, 'Where are we partying tonight then?!'

And then I felt myself thinking, 'What are you doing?! Focus! Focus!' and I came out of that thought and my legs went really heavy. It was like there was a battle going on in there: one bit of my brain was breaking out the party poppers and the other bit was freaking out trying not to hex the whole fucking thing. I had massive peanut butter mouth and wasn't generating any saliva.

And this is the thing with golf. A similar situation in football is being one goal up with five minutes left. But you don't have to be good to hold a one-goal lead with five minutes to go. You don't need to score. You just need to be organised and calm, you need to run down the clock.

You can't run down the clock in golf. You can't even drop back into your own half and boot the ball away every time it comes near you. You have to be aggressive. You have to be at your best. There's nowhere to hide. And now I've got the 17th, one of the hardest holes on the golf course.

It's a par five, and it's a par five with a massive decision to be made. If you get the drive right, you get yourself on the fairway and you're looking at 200 yards to a green that the commentators described as 'an upturned saucer', one that's protected by a big expanse of water. If you don't land on the middle of the green, you'll either roll off the front into the drink or off the back.

The safe thing to do is lay up on the end of the fairway so that your third shot is just a simple chip onto the middle of the green.

But I wasn't in the mood for safe. I didn't see what I had to gain from playing safe. The ball was just on the edge of the rough, but the good stuff, not the deep stuff. And I took the five iron and absolutely smashed it. No danger of landing in the water. For a moment I thought I'd nailed it and landed it on the centre of the green, but the adrenaline has taken it further and it's bounced off and down a steep slope at the back.

Now I'd practised on this green before and it is a bastard. Coming from down the slope, you need some power, but if you give it too much power you'll roll straight past the hole, down the other side and into the water and that's the end of it. My adrenaline was absolutely off the chart. Joost Luiten was one shot and one hole behind me. I took a risk in not just laying it up, but trying to putt up the hill would have been too risky even for me. I got a wedge out and chipped it up onto the green. It broke nicely and rolled up to about seven feet from the hole. That'll do. That'll do nicely. A birdie here would give me a two-shot lead, with a par four on the 18th offering no realistic chance of an eagle.

I missed it. Just overcooked it. It didn't even stop next to the hole for a tap-in. I'd left myself with one of those two footers that feels like a 20-footer. And I had to wait for my partner to put his ball down first. The nerves are something else at this point. I'm just trying to get a grip, trying to control my breathing. I stepped up for my fifth shot. And thank God, it went in. The one-shot lead holds. But the 18th was no picnic either.

The tee shot was decent. I mishit it slightly, but it's on the fairway. I'll take that.

I'd never watched the footage back of this event until I started work on this book. It's weird seeing it now. I can hear how nervous I am, my voice is higher than usual and I sound breathless. Gordy is talking me down.

'It should be a dial-the-number shot,' he says calmly.

'Yeah?' I squeak.

'You don't have to do anything with this club,' he continues. 'If you were going any other way, you'd be going one less, but that five iron at the last has gone 204. You're a little pumped, but this gets there comfortably. You just want to hit it on the TV tower, just left of it, okay? Take your time, stay in the moment, yeah?'

'… yeah.'

But it doesn't quite get there. I didn't hit it hard enough. It bounces just short of the green, down a little slope. I could chip it, but I reach for the putter and go for it. It's 40 feet, so it's just about getting it close. Or maybe getting lucky …

'Take your time now,' says Gordy. 'Just keep doing what you're doing.'

He's right. He was right a lot that week. Gordy was great because he gave straight answers to straight questions. There was no bullshit, there was no eagerness to please, he didn't try to qualify everything he said. He said what he thought. He was the sort of caddie who grabs you round the neck and gives you a shake, who tells you to fucking get on with it.

I take a breath, I give it another long, hard look. And then I hit it. The power is just right, but it's not breaking the way I wanted it to do.

It's not going to go in. But it does stop … it stops about three feet away. I can putt from three feet. Can't I?

I've got a long time to think about it. Both of my playing partners have landed further away, so I have to let them putt first. I'm stalking now. I can't stand still, so I'm prowling around the hole, studying the surface. Is there a slope there? Is there anything I'm missing?

My brain is playing tricks on me. I'm seeing angles that aren't there. And I'm just standing there breathing and I'm thinking, 'You know what? You just need to hit this fucking ball dead straight at the hole.'

I don't remember hitting it. There's nothing there. I just remember picking it back out of the hole and breathing out. But I couldn't celebrate. Joost was right behind me, getting ready to tee off. I've got a par, so if he gets a birdie then we're going to a play-off.

So everyone's cheering and clapping and trying to high-five me and I can't do a thing, I can't say a thing. It's not over. I'm led away by officials and into the scoring shed. Where I have to wait for EIGHT MINUTES to find out how he does. It was insane.

I'm watching this little telly and there's a cameraman behind me, so even though all I want to see is Joost and whether he makes the fairway, I keep seeing the back of my own head. Joost makes the fairway, but his second shot lands with a thump in the bunker to the left of the green.

Now my brain's in freefall. I'm sitting there thinking, 'Oh my God, he's going to put it in from the bunker, isn't he?'

Someone walked in and asked if I was nervous. I tried to play it all down.

'I'm not bothered about that,' I said, waving my hand at the television. 'I want to see the Leicester game!'

Leicester were on their way to their own surprise title win, leaving my Arsenal in their rearview mirror, but I didn't really care about that. All I wanted to see was Joost miss. And I know that sounds bad, but I promise you every single golfer will think the same thing when it comes down to a moment like that.

He hit it well. He hit it really well. From behind him, the ball pops up out of the sand and, for just a moment, it seems to be heading straight for the pin ... and then it falls to the ground, leans to the left and misses by a foot or so.

I have never felt so much relief in my life. And that was the turning point for me. My belief in myself completely changed at that moment. I wasn't the kid who didn't like wearing suits, I wasn't nervously edging myself around the development tours. I wasn't a Challenge Tour player. I was a European Tour player. I was a European Tour *winner*.

If I'd managed that feeling properly, I wonder what could have happened. I wonder how much pain I'd have saved myself. But that was all to come.

In the press conference afterwards, I said that all I wanted to do was to go back to North Mid and get hammered with my mates, which I was able to do a few days later. Weirdly, pictures and videos of that night, with me dressed up as a piñata, ended up in the *Daily Mail*, which is not something I was prepared for. It was the first time that anyone outside of golf had really noticed me. It wouldn't be the last.

But I've got nothing to apologise for. I think it's absolutely normal to want to go and celebrate with your mates at a time like that. Look at Shane Lowry after he won The Open, he was celebrating for a week and it was all cool.

For now, I felt amazing. I felt like everyone treated me differently too. I wasn't just this cuddly 'Beef' guy, I was a winner. I'd won something. I felt like people respected me now. I felt like I could do anything. Three months later I was challenging for The Open. Two weeks after that, I made the cut and tied for 60th at the PGA Championship in New Jersey.

And that's when I discovered that those performances had given me a chance of leaving the European Tour altogether. That's when I realised that I could get myself onto the PGA Tour.

5

FASHION

When you look back at pictures of the early days of golf, you often see pictures of Old Tom Morris, who was known as The Grand Old Man of Golf. Morris is a legend of the game, one of the first legends really. He won The Open four times in the 1860s, he used to play in partnership with his son, Young Tom Morris, and you'll see photographs of the pair of them at loads of golf clubs up and down the country. And all I can think whenever I see them is, how the fuck are you going to swing a golf club dressed like that?

It's insane. They're wearing full-on suits. Like, the whole lot. Heavy trousers, shirts, ties, waistcoats, heavy overcoats. And it's not the sort of suit you'd wear for a summer wedding either. This is really thick material. I don't know how they did it. If I was wearing that, I'd struggle to raise the club for anything more than an awkward chip.

It is fair to say that I am probably not the most fashionable person in sport. Fashion in sport, for me, is all about comfort. I don't want to look good, I want to *feel* good. I don't like any sort of waterproofs, I don't like jackets. If the weather is really bad, I want one of those stretchy things you wear underneath everything, then a T-shirt, a jumper and that's it. Anything else and I feel like I can't move. That's literally my maximum clothing level.

I'm also a man who wants a bit of stretch in his clothes. I'm spending my day bending over, marking my ball, climbing in and out of bunkers, so I need my clothes to be able to cope with that – and it's me, so that means baggy. Fortunately, as the game has just started to relax a little bit, it's easier for me to wear simple stuff. You'll never catch me in a pair of plus fours and a Pringle jumper.

I had a disaster in the 2019 Open, though. I was wearing these trousers that were supposed to be stretchy but they really let me down where it counts. I was warming up before the start and I felt something just go. You know that feeling, when it feels like your trousers have died on you and it all suddenly gets a little bit chilly back there. I got myself back to the golf buggy and assessed the damage. The rip was straight down the middle of my arse, top to bottom, the whole of the moon.

I was in a total panic. It's The Open, you've got TV cameras everywhere and it's not the 1990s. Every single person on the course has got a smartphone and most of them are on social media. I'm about five minutes away from teeing off with a massive fucking tear down my arse and trending on Twitter.

Fortunately, the weather was a little less than summery and I'd packed a pair of waterproof trousers as a just-in-case option.

Unfortunately, they were back in the locker room. I had to call my manager and get him to run over and get them for me. I was begging him to go quickly as well, because I couldn't even stand up without getting myself charged with indecency.

I managed to shuffle myself to this walkway near the first tee, and the guys I was playing with were staring up at me, wondering why I wasn't down there with them. I was trying to signal that I was changing my trousers, but that's a hard message to get across, so everyone just looked really confused. I managed to get my ruined pair off and my waterproofs on as they were calling out my name, and then I had to run down the steps, grab my club and that was it, I was teeing off in The Open. But on the bright side, it really took my mind off any sort of pre-Major nerves and I went up and split the fairway.

I don't wear anything too tight now. I'm traumatised. Let's be honest, no-one wants to see that sort of thing. If I wore the sort of stuff that Rory McIlroy wears, I'd offend everyone. I hate the new trend for tight trousers in golf, the tapered legs that cling to your thighs. I need it baggy.

Rory and I used to play together when we were both amateurs, and when you're young golfers you tend to have a certain type of food in your golf bag. The sort of food that the coaches might not condone. We'd all be out there and I'd be sharing out the Jaffa Cakes and the jelly babies. But as time went on, clearly I was the only fucker who kept eating them. Rory used to have a bit of puppy fat on him, but it's all gone now, he's absolutely ripped, so he can get away with the figure-hugging stuff. But not me. It's best for all concerned if I just keep it baggy.

As the parent of a young child, it's actually best if I don't worry too much about my clothes at all. I've been at tournaments with massive stains on my top and it's because my daughter's tipped a bowl of baked beans over me. You just have to go with stuff like that when you're a parent. And it's nice to have someone else to blame because there have been times when I've bitten into an egg roll and got that dollop of hot yolk down my front.

But while I don't usually think about fashion that much, you do get quite conscious of what you're wearing, especially if you're playing well and you're on the television more. It's not that I want to look good, I just don't want to look like a complete tit.

I always check with my wife everything I pack. She's had some pretty strong views on things I've worn in the past. I used to really like wearing baggy jeans, but she put a stop to that and started picking stuff that was a bit more fashionable.

So I'll have ten shirts, ten pairs of trousers, ten jumpers, and they all get held up for inspection. If she gives me the nod, it's in the suitcase. But there has to be that balance. I don't really care too much what it looks like, I just want to know that it's comfortable.

I'm like that in my normal life too. I live in jeans. Jeans, T-shirt, jumper, pretty basic stuff. I couldn't do a Rickie Fowler and turn up clad head to toe in bright orange sportswear. I just want it simple.

I guess I'm sort of known for my beard more than what I wear, but that was never a deliberate thing. I didn't set out to cultivate a sort of wild man, Robinson Crusoe look. It happened completely by accident.

It was 2015, it was the end of the season, I'd been on the road for a while and I just sort of let it happen. It got to the point where it was no longer stubble, but it wasn't a beard, if that makes sense? A sort of no man's land.

I remember Thomas Bjørn walking up one day and pointing at me, saying, 'What the fuck is that on your face?' and we had a good laugh about it. And I just thought, you know what, I'm not going to shave, I'm just going to let it go and see what happens. So I got Christmas out the way, didn't shave, started the new season, didn't shave, and then out of nowhere I won in Spain and everyone started talking about it.

Most people liked it and it was actually quite useful. I remember playing at the Dunhill once and it was massive by then, a real monster of a beard. It was really windy that day and I didn't have to do that thing where you drop a handful of grass to tell which way it's blowing. I just had to look down at my beard. Of course, the flip side was that it kept getting caught in my jacket zipper. I remember Jon Rahm walking past me and stopping dead.

'Jesus Christ, Beef,' he grinned. 'That is outrageous.'

But not everyone approved. I saw people saying, 'He's got a big bushy beard, it's a terrible image for golf, he's damaging the sport.' How mad is that?

I decided there and then that I was just going to keep growing it out of pure stubbornness. I'm not letting anyone tell me what I can and can't do with my own face. Bad for golf? It's a fucking beard. How can that be bad for golf? It was all so ridiculous that I didn't have any option but to dig my heels in and keep it. And, on the plus side, it did a really decent job of hiding how many chins I had …

Eventually, I did try to shave off the beard and just go with the moustache, which always comes out much blonder and doesn't show up as well. I got the clippers out, cut the beard back to stubble and … God, it looked awful, I couldn't even show my wife. I couldn't even take a picture, it was horrendous. The moustache was all twisty and bendy and my face looked weird.

So I'm stuck with the beard now, but that's okay because I think I've tamed it. I keep it relatively short and neat, I've got a nice length to it and, most importantly, my wife can look at me without laughing. It is strange, though. It started out as an accident, but I've had people send me pictures on social media of them turning up at fancy dress parties in golf gear and a big fake beard. I'll never get used to stuff like that.

You can't talk about fashion in golf without talking about Payne Stewart. He was a fine golfer, he won two US Opens in the 1990s and a PGA Championship too, but if anything he was better known for the way he dressed on the course. He was something else. He was well into his plus fours, those old timey baggy trousers that stop just below the knees. He'd match them up with brightly coloured socks pulled all the way up and then a stylish flat cap on top. Sometimes he'd make it seem quite low key, it would be all browns and tweeds and things. Sometimes it would be bright blue and yellow.

He had a Marmite effect on golf fans; some people loved it and some people hated it. Personally, I think he rocked it. He's probably just about the only person who could have got away with it, but he made it work. Tragically, he was killed in a plane crash in 1999, but I don't think anyone in the sport will ever forget him.

John Daly is in the same category, but in a different way. While Payne's fashion choices were from a different era, by those standards he was very fashionable. John, on the other hand, wouldn't be fashionable in any era. But again; he somehow pulls it off.

He's got trousers that make him look like a can of Beavertown lager and the sort that your elderly aunt would wear to a barbecue. He once went out with Stars and Stripes trousers on. He sometimes looks like he was walking past Primark when it exploded, but it works for him. If I dressed like that, I'd look like an idiot.

The one thing John can't get away with is his original haircut when he first appeared. It was a proper pudding bowl on the top and then a long skinny mullet down the back. What a guy, though, an absolute legend. I've hung out with him a few times and he's something else.

Ian Poulter went through a stage of peacocking too, but I'm not sure he always pulled it off. He's had some absolute shockers in his time. There was one outfit he wore, it was like a gold nylon shirt and straight brown trousers, he looked like he should have been at a 1970s LA roller disco – it was amazing. At one point he dyed his hair blond and then put loads of thick red streaks into it, so he looked like a bowl of raspberry ripple ice cream.

Headgear is a big thing for golfers too. I prefer a simple baseball cap, but one of the big ones, like a trucker's cap. You have to salute Jesper Parnevik for those peaked caps where he pulls the peak right up to the vertical. I've never really understood why he does that, it sort of defeats the object, but he seems happy. I also liked it when he started wearing a pork pie hat because he looked like Mickey Pearce off *Only Fools and Horses*.

I was really impressed with Jarmo Sandelin too. He used to wear these sunglasses that didn't have arms on the side, they went over the top of his head and made him look like a cyborg. You have to respect that.

The one thing I'm really glad about is that golf shoes have changed. We used to have this box at North Mid of all the shoes that people had left in the locker rooms over the years and there were some monsters in there. You know, the ones that are like school shoes with steel spikes on the bottom and these ridiculous flappy leather bits over the laces? I'm so pleased we're not in that era anymore, I couldn't wear anything like that. You can get golf shoes now that look like trainers, they're brilliant. I could wear them to the supermarket and no-one would notice.

As I say, fashion's not really for me. I'm just bothered about the golf. I've never been one to plan an outfit or a look. It just happens naturally. The beard was an accident, the whole 'Beef' thing was a nickname someone else gave me years ago. It's not what it's about. I just want to get out there and hit some golf balls. As long as I'm not wearing a suit, I really don't mind what I'm wearing.

Of course, while I don't like formal dress, there is one blazer that I'd be happy to wear and that's the green blazer you're given when you win the Masters. I'd be more than happy to wear one of those.

And if it ever does happen, I've got the ultimate wind-up planned, because you know how revered those jackets are, right?

The first thing I'll do is get a replica made up. Same colour, same design. No-one will know the difference. And then for the next week or so, all you'll see are pictures of me on a jet ski wearing it, pictures of me in a kebab shop, covered in garlic and chilli sauce, pictures of me quad biking or just standing casually with a load of leaky biros in the top pocket.

It would be amazing. People would be going absolutely crazy thinking that I was destroying this hallowed object.

But ultimately I don't care what I'm wearing. I just want to play golf again. As long as there's a bit of give in the trousers and I'm not going to split them across my arse, I'm happy.

6

THE MAJORS

The Majors are the crown jewels of the golf world. There's only four of them, they're the biggest things you can win, and I absolutely love them. You're got The Open, never the British Open, remember, people get pretty upset about that. It's just The Open. That's the daddy. Actually, that's the granddaddy. When that one started, Queen Victoria still had 41 years left on the throne.

If you win a Major, you write yourself into the history books. You also secure your future too because you lock yourself in on your tour for five years and you get a lifetime invite to that competition. It's amazing, Arnold Palmer played the Masters for fifty years straight, his last one was in 2004 at the age of 75. In 2009, Tom Watson nearly won The Open at the age of 59. You tell me another sport where that happens? Imagine if Gary Lineker turned up at the next World Cup and nearly won the Golden Boot. It's mad.

The atmosphere at a Major is incredible. I actually went to The Open at Royal St George's in 2003 as a fan when I was 13. I was so excited that I even went down for the practice days and was just wandering around watching all of these players that I'd only ever seen on television. It was the first time I saw Tiger Woods. It was wild, there were crowds around him all the time, but I was really taken by the size of him, that athletic build. It was just one of those surreal moments when someone you're only ever seen on the telly is right there. I think I'd have passed out if someone had told me that I'd be playing in the same tournaments as him one day.

I never thought things like that back then. I was just trying to get signatures on my hat and then find the ice cream truck. It was so exciting just to be there. I was like, 'Holy shit! I'm at The Open!' It was wicked.

I remember someone in the crowd there yelling out, 'Ernie Els is going to win it!' I thought that was so strange. Not because Ernie couldn't win, he's one of the best golfers of his generation and he was in great form. But it was just that certainty that got me. It's a Major. Majors aren't like World Cups in football, they're not usually won by the favourites. Anything can happen at a Major. And that was the case in 2003 when Ben Curtis, a complete unknown, won. He doesn't even play golf anymore – he's a coach.

Eight years later, I was there as a player. I had to qualify, I wasn't even on the European Tour at that point. I was still slogging through the Challenge Tour, regaining my confidence. But I wanted to give it a crack. I had to get through a regional qualifier and then a local qualifier. My mate was caddying for me at the regional and we were at the London Club. We got down there early so that I could have a bit of practice and hit some balls. So I did all of that, had a bit of a break, had some lunch and then I said to my mate, 'How long have we got left?'

He said we had 20 minutes, so I thought I'd get a bit of extra time in on the chipping green. So I'm standing there chipping balls around when this guy zips up on a buggy and he's all like, 'What are you doing?! You're supposed to be on the tee!'

I said, 'What are you talking about? We've got 20 minutes!' and I looked at my mate, who was now looking a bit sheepish. His fucking watch had stopped!

I literally ran onto the tee and teed off, it was very nearly a Happy Gilmore! But it didn't affect me at all. I shot five or six under there and then got into the local qualifier two weeks before The Open.

Maybe the late rush to the tees just pushed all the nerves out.

I remember playing really well. It was at the Royal Cinque Ports in Deal. It was tricky, it was really windy, but I was getting myself round okay. I needed to finish in the top four to qualify and I'll never forget the last hole, a par four. It was a long one, and on my second shot I put it in the bunker to the right off the green. That could have been the end of me right there at the last hurdle. But I managed to play the bunker shot of your dreams, the one you pray for when you need it the most. I remember the wedge just cutting through the sand like it was wet loo roll, the ball rising up out of the bunker and just plopping down six inches from the lip of the hole.

And that proved pivotal. I tapped it in and found myself in a four-man play-off for the last two spots.

If you think that's a high-pressure situation, playing off for the right to play in The Open, imagine how it felt when we all made par on hole after hole, the sun went down and we had to call it a day and come back in the morning.

It wasn't easy to get to sleep that night, I tell you. One guy had birdied the first and got through, so there were only three of us battling for one spot. We got back to the course first thing in the morning and it was absolutely dead. It was surreal, standing out there in the morning mist with so much riding on the next hole. And then the other two lads got bogeys and I had two putts from four feet to qualify.

Now, you've got to remember that it's 2011. I'm 22, and at this point I've never played in a big tournament. I've only just got off those Jamega development tours onto the Challenge Tour and I haven't yet played myself onto the European Tour. So this is like going from Sunday League football on Hackney Marshes into the World Cup.

It seemed to take forever for the day to come around. I remember driving up there on the Sunday and seeing all the stands and all the people and I just froze. I felt like a deer in the headlights, it was the most intimidating experience of my life.

The place was just full of all of these people that I'd only ever seen on television. Whichever way I looked, there was another hero. I saw Ben Crane pretty early on, he used to make these golf videos with Rickie Fowler and Bubba Watson, they were really popular at the time, so I had to tell him how much I enjoyed them.

And the thing about The Open is that it is just … open. When you're setting up practice rounds, you just go to the desk and put yourself down for a tee time. So you'd just scroll down the list and see who was playing and then scribble your name down next to them. Rory, Tiger, Bubba, they're all there. I ended up doing a practice round with Tom Watson, who had nearly won the thing just a few years before.

He was lovely, he was really nice to me, but I was a lot shyer in those days and I don't think I asked him enough questions. But you know what? It was enough just to stand next to him and watch him play, to chat with his caddie and see where they were chipping and how they were putting. It was enough just to be there for that.

It was all so crazy. One minute you're playing in a minor event at a small golf course and the next you're having a practice round with a man who's won eight Majors. And you're in this environment where the stands are packed and the atmosphere is incredible.

It all helps too. The crowds on the practice round acclimatise you for the crowds when it all starts on the Thursday. They must have done anyway because I started off really well, got myself a couple under par and I was on the leaderboard. My mates told me that I was on the telly for the 10th hole and then I remember looking up at the board on the side of the green and seeing my name on it. I shit my pants at that point, obviously, but that's to be expected.

I couldn't put the two rounds together. I went round in 74 on the Thursday and for a lot of that round I was one or two under. That was a huge confidence boost for me. I felt that I'd gone out there and shown what I could do. I don't remember much about the 79 on the second round, but that's probably for the best. That was 2011. It took me five years to get back, but when I did it was a very different story.

I qualified in a different way for 2016 at Royal Troon. I was playing well that season, I was sitting in the top 20 for the Race to Dubai, so I qualified automatically. I was also on a bit of a high after that win in Valderrama on the European Tour. I was in a very different headspace. I had experience, I had a trophy and I was just in a completely different place. And even with all of that in mind, I still wasn't ready for my life to be turned completely upside down.

On the first day, I went round in 69. It wasn't in the same class as Phil Mickelson, who did it in 63, but it was a good solid start.

Anything under 70 on the first day is good. You know what they say: you can't win it on day one, but you can certainly play yourself out of it. But then I've gone and done it again on the second day, another 69, and now I've made the cut for the last two days and people are taking notice.

Now I'm going in and signing my scorecard and I'm getting grabbed for interviews by the BBC and Sky. 'What do you think you can do over the weekend?' they're saying and I'm like, 'I haven't even thought about the fucking weekend, I didn't think I'd get here.'

I was paired with Sergio García on the Saturday and walking up to the tee box was just on another level. You walk right under the grandstand and the reception I got just blew me away. Everyone's shouting and screaming and I'm like, 'This is crazy, I'm playing with García,' and they're all shouting about me. I got a 70 there, and while I was still some way behind Mickelson and Henrik Stenson, you never knew how the final day would pan out.

By this point, it's all kicking off. My social media accounts are blowing up, I've got tens of thousands of new followers and the whole 'Beef' thing has caught on. People are shouting it out at me, it's all over the internet. I'm told that the *Guardian*'s online coverage just sort of crossed out 'Johnston' on the scoreboard and replaced it with 'Beef'.

It wasn't just the outside world, though. Strange things were happening even within my own family. I remember chipping one in and trying to stay cool, you know, trying to keep myself on a level. I picked the ball out of the hole and walked over to the side of the green where my sister was standing. She said, 'Look what you've done! You've made your mum cry!' and there's my mum in floods of tears. I was like, 'Fucking hell. I can't deal with that today.' I just literally had to turn away and walk off. I had to shut it down because I can't have those emotions in the middle of a round. It sounds cold to just shut down on your mum like that, but I would have gone to pieces.

I walked out on the Sunday, still in contention for a big finish, and I was a bit more ready for it. But I still couldn't quite believe it was real. I was like, 'Holy shit, man. What the fuck is going on here?' I needed to just take a moment and settle myself down. I was playing in a tournament, but there was so much stuff outside, it was hard to focus. It's a cliché, but it was genuinely a life-changing moment for me.

I kept thinking about this guy from North Mid, Freddy George. He was the local pro there and when I was growing up I used to look up to him in awe. They had pictures of him on the wall, he'd played in two Opens. I used to stare at them and think, 'Fuck, that guy is incredible.' And then suddenly I'm there, not just in my second Open, but sitting there on the final day in the top ten. That's nuts.

Even now when I think about it after eight years, I can't quite believe it.

So I go out there on the Sunday, I walk underneath that grandstand, I know exactly what's going to happen ... and it still blows me away. As soon as I'm there, I've got a camera in my face and everyone's going crazy. I'm nervous, really fucking nervous, but I get out there and I start to settle. I've hit two shots on the first and I've got myself a 30-foot putt. It's a tough one, but someone's played that shot from a similar place and I've been watching and I think I've got a really good read of it. So I just said to myself, 'I'm going to make all these people go nuts with this shot. I've seen the line, I know what to do here,' and I just … I never felt like that ball would do anything else other than go in the hole. And I hit the shot, down it went and it felt like the world exploded around me.

It was *so* much fun. That's the thing I always remember about it, even more so because of what happened afterwards and how bad it all got. But at this point, fun was the only word for it all. Just knocking it in and making all those people go crazy. I had three birdies in the first four holes and suddenly I'm sat there in third place.

I couldn't quite hang on, though. I bogied the 8th and then three more bogies followed on the back nine. I was in one of the last groups, so there was so much attention on us as we went round. The stands were packed and when I walked out onto the 18th, even though I'd slipped down the leaderboard, the crowd were still incredible. I'll never forget that. If I lived to be a hundred, I don't think I'd ever have a feeling like that again. I was at the next one in 2017, but it wasn't like that. That week at Troon was spooky. And, as you'll read later, what followed wasn't always good.

I think the bigger events suit me, though. I don't know why, but they seem to sharpen my focus. I love the big occasion, it seems to ease the pressure and anxiety. And that's what's driven me on while I've been out injured; the thought of getting back to them.

There's nothing like a Major, they're the greatest events to play in and I just want to be back there.

Of course, The Open isn't the only Major. The US Open is something special too. That's a different ball game entirely. I've played three of those and they are the hardest test for any golfer. If you win one of them, you must be doing something right.

The courses are so difficult. I played Oakmont in 2016. I'd heard it was a difficult course. I didn't know the half of it. I played nine practice holes on the Sunday, another nine on the Monday. It was fucking unplayable. You see it sometimes on the telly, they're watering the greens in between groups because the sun has baked them out and the surface is like ice, they're just so fast.

The 17th is a short par four up the hill. You can hit a driver and get on the green if you do it right, but if you miss it, you're going to be in so much bother. I tried a few irons off the tee to play it safe. I was saying to my caddie, 'They can't have this on the Thursday, they're going to have to water the greens or no-one will stay on them.' When we walked up there, they were watering the rough too, so it was double trouble. Hit the green and whizz straight off it or hit the rough and vanish into the jungle. Seriously, you wander off the fairway there and you can't even see your shoes. When you get to the US Open, it's not a game of golf, it's a game of chess – you're having to think about every single shot.

That tournament, they had a massive thunderstorm, buckets and buckets of rain. If that hadn't happened, that event would go down as the worst US Open in history. The cut would have been twelve over. As it was, it was six over with soft, wet greens.

At most golf courses, you can drop a ball onto a green with a pitching wedge and it will stop dead. At Oakmont, the shortest distance I could make a ball stop was 13 yards. So you are just playing for the front edge of the green every single time. And even then people were putting it straight off the other side. It was so, so hard. Dustin Johnson won that one. He was one of only four golfers to finish the tournament under par. If it hadn't have been for that thunderstorm, no-one would have managed it.

I've done three US Opens and they've all been that hard. They're fun in a way, but they're a really stressful challenge. It's very easy to make a six or a seven anywhere on the course.

In 2017 at Erin Hills they made all the holes longer to try to stop the scoring. I think that one was nearly 7,800 yards in total, which was crazy. But it was still easier than Oakmont.

I came 42nd in that one. I never quite got myself in contention, but 42nd in a US Open is still a pretty decent week's work. It's the finest of margins but you enjoy the battle.

And then you've got the PGA Championship and you know the old joke about that one? You've got The Open and you love it for the history and the US Open you love it for the challenge and the Masters you love it for Augusta and the PGA Championship no-one gives a fuck. People really say that.

But it's the strongest field you'll get in golf. It's basically the top 100 golfers on the planet at any given time, but like The Open, there's still a bit of room for the unknowns. All the club professionals under the PGA have the chance to qualify and, just as it was for me at Troon in 2016, it can be a life-changing experience for people.

Michael Brock had that in 2023 – he hit a hole in one, finished tied for 15th and suddenly he's signed with an agency and playing in big tournaments.

The only one I've never played is the Masters. That one goes on world ranking. I was close through 2016 and 2017, but I just missed the cut-off. That's on the list. That's one of the things that's driving me on. I've got to play Augusta.

Even people who don't like golf, like the Masters. I've never heard a bad thing about that course. Everyone loves it. That's where Tiger made his name and that's where I need to be.

7

THE PGA TOUR

If you had to put it into football terms, the PGA Tour is the Premier League and the Champions League rolled into one. It's the toughest tour with the greatest players playing week in and week out. Everyone wants to be on it and I was no exception.

The European Tour has some brilliant events and the crowds are great. On the PGA Tour *every* event is enormous. It's big every single week. How could you not want to be a part of that?

I don't regret joining the tour in 2017. I regret delaying my start and sticking around to finish the European Tour first. That cost me crucial points. I regret not staying in the USA after I inevitably failed to retain my tour card. I could have earned it back on the Korn Ferry Tour, which would have been well within my abilities.

I wish I'd had my coach with me too. He had other commitments in Europe and couldn't come with me. I'm the sort of player who needs a coach to bounce off, someone who can calm me down and put things right before they go really wrong. Sometimes you can feel that there's something slightly off with your game and it's good to sit down with a coach, get the launch monitors out and together you can work on it. So I regret that he wasn't there.

I still had Gordy, my caddie, and he was fully in favour of heading out there, but it wasn't long before he started to get the hump. He could see that I was struggling. He felt that I wasn't being managed right, I was spending too much time doing media stuff and not enough practising. And he was probably right. I certainly wasn't playing as well as I had in the past. He wanted me on the putting greens, but I was always off being interviewed. It was my fault. I should have gone straight over as soon as I got the tour card. I should have given myself time to settle.

I didn't even know it was possible for me to get my tour card so quickly. Two weeks after The Open, I went and played in the PGA Championship and I made the cut, finishing tied for 60th. I'd already made the cut for the US Open earlier in the season and what I didn't know was that these finishes all counted as points for the PGA Tour as well as the European. I'd done well enough over the three Majors to make myself eligible for the Korn Ferry Play-Offs. A few good performances across those tournaments could push me over the threshold, so I had a decision to make. Do I stick around and work on my European ranking, trying to finish as high as possible up the board, or do I have a crack in the States? I was like, 'Fuck it, man, let's go over there! Let's go and play!'

So I went out to Ohio, made the cut, but finished pretty low down. Then I went to this small town in Idaho called Boise. It was a wicked little place, really small, but great people and loads of craft beer breweries. I finished fourth there and that was enough, I had a PGA Tour card!

The European Tour weren't massively keen on me going and I'd already had a bit of a row with them that year. I'd qualified for the World Golf Championship and it was the same weekend as the French Open, a pretty big event for the tour. They hit the roof, they were furious and they were doing everything they could to convince people to stay and play. They offered double points: they made it count double for the big-name players to reduce their obligations to play in other events. Lots of them stayed, but I didn't know if I'd ever get invited to another World Championship and I wanted to play.

They weren't having it. They said, 'We'll fine you if you play,' and so, again, I had a decision to make. I chose to tell them to go fuck themselves. 'Do what you want, I'm never paying you a fine, fuck you!' I'm not having anyone pressurise me into not playing a tournament. It's a World Golf Championship, it's at Firestone, a legendary course, and I wanted to go and experience that.

So having come through all of that, I don't think I made myself too popular by saying I was heading off to try my luck in the States.

Because of that win in Spain, I was pretty safe. I had a two-year exemption as long as I came back and played at least four events a year. But I should have just gone out straightaway instead of sticking around to play in Turkey, South Africa and Dubai. I really needed that time in the USA to settle in and get my bearings.

The differences were clear right from the start. Don't get me wrong, the European Tour is great, there are some fantastic events, but the PGA Tour is just a step above. You know how everyone says that everything in America is bigger? Well, this was absolutely the case.

You'd fly in for a tournament, get your bags and there would be people at the airport at a stand with a big banner for whatever the event was. You'd wander over there and say hello, they'd check you in and then they'd give you the keys to a car for a week. And it wasn't just any car. It would always be one of the sponsors' cars, so it would be a massive SUV, or a flash BMW or, at one event, a fucking F-150 truck. It was amazing.

On the European Tour, you'd be at the little Avis branch having the usual row with the manager. 'This ain't a Category C car, this is a Citroën Berlingo! What happened to the car from the picture, mate? Oh, you've run out of them, have you?'

In the States you'd just take the keys, drive off to your hotel, play your golf and drop the keys back at the airport on your way back home. And when you got to the hotel, they'd have a whole list of local restaurants, local events, they'd be giving you tickets for stuff, it was insane. You want your clothes washed? Hand them in at the locker room, they'll be ready for you the next day. No more washing my pants in the tiny sink in my hotel!

Everything changed. They had an electronics allowance, so if you wanted a new iPad to film your swing, you got $2,000 for that, it was just so far out.

But it was the simple things that made the difference. When you're on the European Tour, they've got a players' lounge, but they're really strict on the access. I've had a few rows over the years when my mum and my brother have come to see me play, but I've been told I can only let one of them in at a time. It's mad, my mum gets to one or two events a year and I can't take her for a cup of tea? In the USA, it's completely different. They've got a players' lounge, they've got a family dining room, everything is just … bigger.

Including, unfortunately, my scores. The first tournament I played was at Torrey Pines and I was just horrible there. I only missed the cut by three, but I played really, really badly. I was just miles off where I should have been.

The hype was off the charts, but I couldn't match it with a decent performance. It was so frustrating. People were treating me like a hero, but I was playing so poorly. I found the treatment quite hard to deal with, and it was not long before it was just flat-out awkward.

The first sign of it came when I played with Scott Piercy at the PGA Championship. It was New Jersey, so it was loud and rowdy throughout, properly fucking crazy, and all these people were shouting, 'BEEF! BEEF! BEEF!' And it's great, you know, I love the support and I was just really happy that people were happy, but it was beginning to piss everyone else off. I was getting a few looks, if you know what I mean.

The reporters kept asking players what it was like to play with me, which is ridiculous. It was no surprise when Scott just snapped at one of them. 'I think I've had enough of Beef for one day,' he said.

It was all completely out of my control. I had to be careful where I walked because wherever I went, people would start shouting and it would put the other players off. Some of the best players, the guys at the absolute top of the game, found it quite amusing.

Some of the others really didn't. And there was nothing I could do about it. If I was backing it up with results, it might have been bearable. But I wasn't.

I was tied for 10th in Puerto Rico in March 2017, my best finish on the tour, but it didn't feel that way. I was two shots off the lead at one point and then I missed the green out of the bunker with a truly horrible shot, bogeyed, and then blew the last three holes and any chance of a top-five finish. It was one of my strongest overall performances, but it really knocked my confidence. I missed the cut in Houston a week later.

It was so difficult to handle. In some ways, it's almost worse to just squeeze through the cut. You end up teeing off at 7 a.m. on the Saturday and the Sunday, and, while anything can happen on a round of golf, you know that even this sport isn't so fucking crazy that you can power through from there and make a good finish. If you're in the 30s and you have a good last day, anything's possible, but it's not like that if you're squeezing through all the time.

I had a smile on my face in New Orleans, though. What a place that is, what a cool week. It was a team event, so I was playing fourballs and foursomes with Kyle Reifers, a lovely bloke. The only downside was that Jazz Fest was on at the time and because of a combination of tee times and thunderstorms, we never got to go out and see any of the bands I wanted to see.

But it was great, I did lots of bits of media about the different food they have there, I was getting dragged around and asked to try all this amazing stuff. I found a pub there called The Bulldog and that was a proper giggle, I loved it in there. The people were great too. Lots of them were coming up and asking for pictures, and I was really happy to do it, but I was starting to feel weird about it. I was beginning to feel like I shouldn't be there, that my golf wasn't good enough for the sort of attention I was getting.

I didn't feel homesick, but I didn't exactly feel at home either. I felt like I wanted to get away. I went back to Europe for a few tournaments. I got some much-needed time with my coach and I started to improve again, but I split with Gordy. I could tell he wasn't happy, we spoke about it and just agreed to go our separate ways.

I had a few decent results after I came back: tied for 21st at the BMW PGA in Surrey, tied for 42nd at a brutal US Open, 19th in Scotland, God I love Scotland, and then tied for 21st at The Open before doing my shoulder in at the PGA Championship.

It was the very first round and I noticed that I was struggling to get the speed up in my swing. It wasn't painful, but it felt a bit tight and so I was trying to work around it. Then all of a sudden, I had this hideous pain at the top of my back swing and I was done. I couldn't continue and I had to withdraw. That was me done for nearly three months.

I played in a few of the last European Tour events, made some decent scores, and then I came back to the USA and played in the RSM Classic. And I'll tell you how that went in a later chapter, but it's a story that involves me chucking clubs in the swamp, so there's a clue for you.

That turned out to be the end of the adventure. I had a medical exemption that would have allowed me to play more tournaments, I had the opportunity to quickly win my card back on the Korn Ferry, but I was in such a bad place by then that I didn't take the opportunities. I just went home.

Everything started to go wrong then. But to speak about that properly, we need to take a step back and return to 2016.

8
FAME

There are some nuggets of advice that you don't ever expect to be given in life. 'Be careful with all of those high-fives' is right up there at the top of the list. I would never have expected a simple high-five to be considered an occupational hazard, but when I suddenly ended up in the limelight in 2016, more than a few well-known golfers contacted me to tell me to be careful.

I couldn't help myself. For a while, every time I walked from one hole to another, the way was lined with well-wishers, all shouting, 'BEEEEEEEF!' and holding out their hands for a celebratory slap. And I'm not kidding, it was *every* hole. People got in touch and said, 'You've got to be careful, mate. It only takes one person to get over-excited, injure your hand and then you've got problems.'

I really took it to heart and started to tuck my thumb in a bit so there wouldn't be as much impact on the muscle. And people were really good. They'd just dangle their hands out, I'd give them a friendly knock as I went by, it was all cool. I'm fairly sure it's not the reason I've been out of the game for so long with a thumb injury, but you do wonder sometimes.

I was so completely unprepared for what happened that year that I'm almost surprised I came through it mostly normal. It wasn't easy, and I'll discuss some of the bleaker moments later in the book, but it's probably enough for now for me to say that I always try to keep an eye out for younger people going through the same thing. It's too much.

It started out just fine. After that amazing final day at The Open, I did a load of media work and then spent about an hour and a half posing for pictures with people, signing autographs and I loved it, it was great fun. Then I finally got to the players' lounge and spent a good few hours in there. The adrenaline was still pumping so hard, so it didn't matter how many drinks I poured down myself, I couldn't unwind. I had family friends there and we slipped out and went to a bar near my Airbnb, had even more drinks and then stayed up until gone 4 a.m. just hanging out and chatting around the kitchen table.

The next day I had a pretty sizeable hangover, so doing a 10 a.m. interview with Sky Sports wasn't ideal, but I came through that with the help of a sausage sandwich and a can of Irn-Bru. And that was in the good old days before they took all the sugar out of it. Life saver. I'm terrible for hangovers, I get so dehydrated that all I want to do is just dunk my head into a bowl of cold water. That morning, I could have just walked out into the North Sea, I'd have been more than happy with that.

But the interview was fine, it was actually good fun to just look back on the tournament and have a laugh about it all. But things started to change that same day. At some point over the week, someone had asked what sort of music I liked and I'd said something about Scroobius Pip. And all of a sudden I was getting messages from him on Twitter. He's a lovely bloke and it was wonderful, but that's not really a normal thing to happen to a normal person.

Then we stopped at a service station on the way home, and people were coming up and asking for pictures and autographs. And again, it was lovely, but when I was back in the car, sitting in the back seat, I was just thinking to myself, 'This is all nuts.'

I'd won in Spain and that was great, I was starting to get a bit of a name for myself in the golf world. But The Open wasn't confined to the golf world. The Open is mainstream, it was on the BBC. All of a sudden, I seemed to have got a name for myself with everyone. And it didn't fade away.

One of the first things I did afterwards was go to this chicken wing festival in London, Wing Fest, and that's not, you'd assume, a natural home of hardcore golf fans. But it was the same thing there, crowds of people wanting pictures and autographs and high-fives and a chance to chat. And I didn't resent any of it, it was all good, but it was just … I wasn't used to it all. I understood it at a golf course, but this was a chicken wing festival.

It happened so quickly and I didn't have a chance to do anything other than just go with it. So I was all like, 'Cool, take a picture.'

I didn't know why they wanted a picture, but sure, take a picture. It wasn't a bad situation at that point, it was just really, really weird.

And not just for me. There were people I'd been friends with for ages, they just knew me as Beef from the golf club, and suddenly all this is happening and complete strangers are wandering up in the pub wanting selfies. It was a big change.

It made everything uncertain too. I felt a bit vulnerable and I was always wary when I left the house. How was I dressed? What sort of mood was I in? Did I have anything stuck in my teeth?

Have a think about the last seven days of your life. Have you, at any point in the last week, been in a bad mood, or been a bit short with someone? Were you a bit off with the cashier when you'd been in a long queue at Asda? Or just a bit quiet and withdrawn?

Did you tut at someone on the bus? Did you give someone a funny look? We all have bad days, we all have those moments where we're not exactly our best selves, but now I felt that if I wasn't on sparkling form, if I wasn't the 'Beef' that everyone thought they knew and I was just 'Andrew Johnston', that it would end up on Twitter.

And that's just the innocuous stuff. What about all the things I did after a few pints? What if someone recorded me babbling away at the bar? What would happen the

around staring at me, like, 'What the hell is going on?' All I could do was just shrug at them. I didn't have a fucking clue.

I was at a tournament in New Jersey and it was properly intense. New Jersey has got a bit of reputation anyway for being a bit rowdy, but this was on a different level. Every tee, every green, everywhere I went, it was going crazy. People don't really shout that much in the UK, but in New Jersey, it's just relentless, everyone's just bellowing 'BEEEEEEEF!' at me wherever I go.

There were lots of careful high-fives there.

I got on the PGA Tour and some sports channel did a poll on who people were most excited to see that season. I was above Tiger Woods. It was, like, what the actual fuck? Like literally, what is going on?

I've won a tournament on the European Tour, that's great. I've had a decent finish in a Major, that's great too. My game is going in the right direction, but I wasn't anywhere near people like Tiger. I wasn't close to anyone. And that's when the imposter syndrome really started to kick in. But it hadn't started to bite by that point.

More on that later.

There was still time for some good stuff, though. I was practising in the USA, working with Claude Harmon at a golf course called the Floridian, and I rocked up in my hire car and parked next to this gorgeous yellow Ferrari. And this golf club is amazing, it's one of the really exclusive ones, and when you arrive they have someone drive a buggy to your car to pick you up. It's wild. So this guy comes along and he puts my clubs onto the back of the buggy and he says, 'You picked a spot here. That's Michael Jordan's car.'

I went in and had breakfast with Claude and told him who I was parked next to, you know, basically one of the greatest sportsmen who has ever lived. And he was really cool about it. Surprisingly cool.

'Do you want to meet him?' he said, as if he was talking about introducing me to his accountant.

And I was like, 'Yeah, of course! As long as we're not in his way or anything.'

So we're out on the range hitting a few balls and Jordan comes around to the hole next to us. Claude says, 'Come on, let's walk over and say hi.'

So we walk over to where he's parked his buggy and literally, before I can even say anything, he's looked up and said, 'Hey! What's up, Beef?'

And I am like, 'No way. No way. No fucking way does he know who I am.'

So I tried to play it cool, I said, 'All right, Michael, how's your golf today?' and we had a bit of a giggle, watched him tee off and I said, 'Have a good one, man,' and he turned back and said, 'You too, Beef. You too.'

That was so weird. But one of the nicest people I met was Kunal Nayyar who played Raj on *The Big Bang Theory*. I was playing in the Pebble Beach Pro-Am and I was sitting there watching telly a few weeks beforehand and I got a message from him asking if I wanted to play with him and if I wanted to go for a practice round.

Now I'd never watched *The Big Bang Theory*, but he seemed like a nice bloke and I said, yeah sure, of course, man, let's do it. And we weren't able to find the time for a round, but we met up a couple of times and had a chat and I told him that I was heading out to Los Angeles soon.

He said, 'If you're down that way, give me a call and we can play at my local course.' So I gave him a call.

He said that he'd set up a fourball for us with Alfonso Ribeiro, who played Carlton in *The Fresh Prince of Bel-Air*, and Justin Timberlake. So that was pretty random.

Justin had to pull out sadly, but it was such a cool day, just hanging out and playing golf with two super-famous sitcom stars. And they were so nice, they really looked after me. We went out to dinner a few times, Kunal took me to his favourite restaurant and now we keep in touch all the time. If he's over in London, we meet up; if I'm over there, we stay in touch. They're just the nicest people.

And, no, I didn't ask Alfonso about Will Smith or life on *The Fresh Prince*. By this point I'd become aware that people always want to ask you the same questions when they meet you, so discussing their TV shows was the last thing I was going to bring up over dinner. We just talked about golf and life. But Kunal did invite me to come over and watch a recording of *The Big Bang Theory*, and that was amazing, seeing how good they are at what they do.

I ended up getting to know Aaron Ramsey too, when he was playing for Arsenal. As a Gooner, that worked out pretty well. We met at The Grove and played there in a pro-am, and he said that if I ever wanted a ticket for a game I should just drop him a line.

But I wasn't sure about that. I'm one of those people who just won't ever ask, I don't know why. So eventually he just offered me a seat in his box for a Champions League game. He took me down to pitch side after the game, it was amazing.

We watched a game together once, when he was out injured, and he was sat there marvelling at how big it all looked from up above the pitch. He said that when you're down there playing, it feels like there's no room for anything, there's no time to think, you get closed down so quickly, so everything has to be done at full speed. But when you're up in the stands, you can see all this open space and gaps to operate. It's funny how every sport seems different when you're actually out there doing it.

Arsenal were in the FA Cup final in 2017 against Chelsea, but I wasn't sure if I could go because I was playing an event at Wentworth. But I thought to myself; if I don't make the cut, I'll go to the game. If I do make the cut and I'm playing on Saturday, I might have an early tee time, so I'll go round the course and then get over to Wembley. And if I had a late tee time, then I was obviously doing really well and it was probably best to focus on that.

I met Aaron a few days beforehand and me, him and my brother were out to dinner and we were talking about goal celebrations. I mentioned that I used to play the trumpet when I was a kid and he thought it was really funny. He said, 'If I score in the cup final, I'll do a little trumpet celebration for you.'

I had a great Friday, went round in 68 and made the cut, so there was no chance of making it to the Cup Final. I didn't even make it off the course in time to see the kick-off in the clubhouse. But I was watching when he thundered in and scored the winner with a header and me and my brother went mad. And then, when he'd finished celebrating with the crowd, he turned to the camera and did a little trumpet thing with his fingers. Me and my brother went mad all over again, no-one knew why we were going crazy. I texted him straight after the game and said, 'Mate, you absolute joker!'

That was incredible. And it was the best of those mad little moments with celebrities. You eventually realise that they're all just normal people, they're not there to be put on a pedestal or anything. They get idolised and worshipped, but when you talk to them they're just normal dudes who do the same stupid shit we all do to make our mates laugh.

But it wasn't long before the backlash started. Almost exactly a year from when it all started, to be precise. I was at Birkdale later that year for the 2017 Open and I'd been playing okay again. I'd made the cut, I was on with Adam Scott on the Saturday and I … well, I'd managed the golf ball, if you know what I mean.

I hadn't played well, but I'd got it round and I'd got it round a couple of shots under par, which felt like a bit of a miracle given some of my shots. I was frazzled, I was tired, I was feeling a lot of pressure and I came into the locker room, turned my phone on and it just blew up with messages.

It's really confusing when that happens. By this point, I was used to having a few notifications on my Twitter every time I logged back on, but this was way more than usual, it was in the thousands. So you're staring at the phone like an idiot thinking, 'What the fuck's happened? I haven't been playing particularly well, but I haven't been really bad either ... did I say something offensive without realising it?'

What you get when you're at the centre of a Twitter storm is just thousands of out of context messages, all these people weighing in and having arguments that you know must have something to do with you because you're tagged into them, but you have to keep scrolling and reading until you can put all the pieces together.

It turned out that some radio presenter had been mouthing off about me, taking the piss out of the way I looked and asking if I was an embarrassment to the sport. They were really going for it, calling me 'Beef the Teeth' and just tearing me to pieces for no reason. They even did a poll to see if they could rally people to agree that I really was a clown.

I was furious. Even when I think about it now, I'm still angry about it. I don't mind a bit of criticism, I understand that it comes with the job. You can have an opinion on the way I play, but there's a line, there's no need to make it so personal and if you do that, I'm going to bite back.

When I look back now at what I typed, I'm actually surprised that I kept my shit together.

'If I'm a clown for enjoying my work, then so be it. You're a sad person and I couldn't care less what you think.'

That wasn't what I wanted to type. I wanted to type, 'Fuck off, you bunch of pricks.'

They were calling me a one-hit wonder, and as that's exactly what I was starting to think about myself it really struck a nerve. I shouldn't have replied at all. I was still in the locker room, for fuck's sake. I shouldn't have had the phone out, I hadn't had time to decompress after the round. But it was just fuel to the fire that was burning inside me anyway.

And it was all going off on there. Unless you've been at the centre of something like this, you can't know what it's like to just have this relentless line of complete strangers weighing in and passing judgement as you're literally holding the phone in your hand. It's like they're in the room, in your life, picking you to pieces.

Some people were great, Thomas Bjørn and Sir Nick Faldo were piling in and supporting me, and some people are going the other way and joining in with the mockery. And that's exactly what the fucker wanted, wasn't it? He wanted to have a pop at me and get a load of publicity for himself. He was just lucky that he wasn't at the golf course that day because, the mood I was in, I would have smeared him across the wall.

Like I said earlier, I'm not one for fighting. I never have been. I think I'm a nice enough guy, I've got respect for other people and I try to be a good man. But when someone crosses that line with me, the red mist comes down and it stays down. For ages afterwards, I was desperate for our paths to cross so that I could put him on his arse.

People were getting in touch that night as it was happening, sending me messages, 'Beef, you've got to let it go, you need to calm down.'

Instead, I just got caught up in a proper back and forth with him. And with all-comers. It felt physical, I felt I was being ganged up on, that I was forced into a corner. I just wanted to keep swinging at people until they all fucked off.

And again, that was exactly what he wanted and the last thing I needed on the night before the final day at The Open. I finished tied for 27th and the media on the final day barely asked me a single question about the golf. All they wanted to talk about was the Twitter spat.

I hate even thinking about that day. I should have just ignored it. It's just Twitter, it doesn't even mean anything. I know that now. Social media is absolute crap, it's meaningless, almost no-one there has got a fucking clue what they're talking about. But that's the learning curve. You don't know these things when you get into it, you just find out the hard way. You've got no idea, you've had no preparation, you've got no protection. And if they catch you on a bad day, you end up like me; playing their little game for them

When Fallon Sherrock, the darts player, was tearing up the sport, going further than any woman had ever gone in the PDC World Championships, I sent her a message. I said, 'Make sure you've got good people around you, people who can protect you and keep your feet on the ground.'

Because I know what it's like. I know how quickly it can all change and how the same people who were cheering for you when you were at your best will be ripping you to pieces if you don't meet their expectations. Look at the way people went for Emma Raducanu after she won the US Open but didn't get past the second round in subsequent Majors. She was a teenager and she was getting absolutely hammered. Look at Bukayo Saka. Everyone was loving him, and then he missed a penalty in the final of the European Championships and he's getting dog's abuse.

I don't blame anyone for it, it's just life. It's just what people do and we should have been ready for it. Shaun, my manager at the time, was just as out of his depth as I was back then. Neither of us knew what we were doing or how to handle what was coming. I think he'd say the same thing too. I'm sure there are things we both wish we could have done differently. It was just an absolute whirlwind and we weren't ready for it.

These days, I've more level-headed. After an experience like that, you have to take what you can from it. I know who I am, I know what I am, I've got an incredible family, I've got good friends. You can say what you want about me. It means absolutely nothing. But I wish I'd known that in 2017.

9

DARK PLACES

I never knew that I was struggling with my mental health. I don't think people always do. It's the sort of thing that can just creep up on you, even when you're giving yourself little clues that things might not be quite right. Like power drinking on your own. Or furiously hurling your golf clubs up trees. Or walking off the course and giving serious thought to never coming back.

Looking back now, it's easy enough to diagnose what happened and why. But I never even saw it coming.

Everything was happening too quickly. Life was too wild. The entire period from the summer of 2016 to the end of 2017 felt like about a month. A mad, relentless month of golf and celebrity and pressure and absolute fucking chaos. No-one around me could see that I wasn't coping at all, that I needed to take a step back. And so what happened happened, one self-destructive step at a time.

Things were just happening too fast for all of us. Me, my manager, my caddy, my girlfriend at the time. We were always travelling, too deep in it to realise what was going on, if that makes sense?

I was at a PGA tournament in 2017, the RSM Classic that I mentioned earlier, at the Sea Island golf club. I was carrying a shoulder injury that had caused me to pull out of the PGA Championship a few weeks earlier and I'd had a painkilling injection just to get me on the course. I wasn't playing well at all, I shouldn't have been anywhere near a golf course. I just wasn't in the right frame of mind.

It's funny, it's so easy to see the problem now, but at the time I was just obsessed with trying to keep up with the best players. I'd finished in the top ten at The Open, hadn't I? I *should* be keeping up with the best players. I should be up there with the likes of Phil Mickelson and Rory McIlroy and maybe even Tiger too. I was judging myself against everyone. I used to play with Rory and he's won three Majors. Why haven't I won three Majors?

I set myself impossible targets and then lost the plot when I inevitably fell short of them. I was just playing worse and worse, and then I'd literally tear up and hit another bad one and I'd be fucking livid. It was like this awful negative feedback loop, everything I did made it worse.

I played horrible on the first day at Sea Island and so I went out early in the morning on day two for a bit of practice on the first tee. I knew it pretty well. There's a massive hazard that runs all the way down the left side and the wind was coming off the right. So I was hitting these shots with the driver, sending the ball out to the right into the wind where it would hold up nicely and drift back in. I must have hit ten or fifteen of those shots, putting the ball just where I wanted every single time.

So when I get up on the first tee for real, I'm expecting to nail it. Why wouldn't I nail it? I've just done it again and again and again with no problems. And then I fuck it up and I put it straight down the left into the hazard.

I'm one shot into the round and my head's already gone. The blood is up, the hands are sweaty, I'm marching down the course in a fucking rage already. So I drop the ball down next to the hazard and look up towards the tee. It's an easy shot. You can't miss the green if you aim to the right of the pin. You can't miss the green if you aim to the right of the pin. I missed the green.

I turned around and hurled my nine iron up this massive fucking great fir tree. It's probably still up there now, rusting in the branches. So now I've been out there for about three minutes and I'm on my fourth shot and I'm one club down. Twenty minutes later, I'm two clubs down; my three wood is sinking into swampy marshland and I have lost my shit completely. I can't be comforted, I can't be spoken to. I'm in total rage mode.

My caddie is just staring at me, but he's not going to say anything. No-one does when it goes like this. He's just thinking, 'No win bonus for me today then.' He's completely helpless. And I cannot get off the golf course quick enough. I don't care what I say or what I do in the meantime.

People must have looked at me like I was a right dick-head. But this is golf. This can happen. We've all seen it in other people. You shake your head and you let them get it out of their system. You don't intervene. You leave them to it. If someone had tried to put an arm around me, I'd have torn it off. If you'd have given me a hammer, I'd have looked for stuff to smash to pieces. It was a full-on temper tantrum. Fuck it. Fuck it all. I don't give a shit. Stupid fucking sport. Get me off the course.

It's like a toxin in your system, poisoning everything. And it hangs around. Usually I love speaking to people at a tournament, I'm always happy to have a chat or pose for a picture, but if anyone had approached me that day, and I don't think they did, I don't think anyone would have been brave enough, they wouldn't have got anything from me. I felt like a fraud. I would have shouted at them, 'Why are you even talking to me? I'm shit at golf, go talk to someone good.'

I was out of the clubhouse that day almost immediately, straight into my car and out of the car park. Get me the fuck out of this place. And as soon as I was away from the golf course, I started to calm down.

But then, even though I'd think that I was okay, that I was centred again, I continued to make things worse. I didn't do any of the stuff that you're supposed to do after a round of golf. I didn't stretch, I didn't eat well, I didn't decompress.

What I did do was go and have a few pints. And then I'd find some food. Some really good, but really bad food, if you know what I mean. I'd be out on the hunt for a barbecue place, a pile of red meat and a load of beer to wash it down. And I'd think it was just a bad day at the office. I'd think I was okay. But I really wasn't okay.

In 2018, I was at the US Open, a really tough tournament at Shinnecock Hills. I played well on the first couple of days, two 73s on a brutal course. If I'd replicated that sort of performance across the four days, I could have finished in the top 20. But I got an 83 on the Saturday and it was an absolute horror show. Shit golf.

Sometimes a drink can really help you after a bad day, It helps you unwind, you have a chat with people, you might even have a laugh about it all. This was not one of those times.

I marched into the players' lounge and ordered a pint, a glass of red wine and a glass of white wine. Saw them, wanted them, smashed all three of them back and then ordered the same again. And I still didn't think I had a problem. Funny, isn't it? It should have been obvious. Who orders that round for themselves? Even teenage drinkers know that you don't mix grape and grain. It's an act of self-destruction. There's no other reason you would order and down those drinks.

People were saying, 'Are they all for you?' And I was just like, 'Yeah. So fucking what? Are you telling me not to drink? Fuck off.'

People tried to talk to me, but I wasn't there for it. 'Fuck off. I'm having a drink. Leave me alone.'

My caddie had to intervene at 9 p.m., by which point I was absolutely battered and had to be guided back to my bed. An absolute fucking mess.

It was all so stupid. I should have been having the time of my life. I was only a few years on from those Jamega competitions and the Challenge Tour. I should have lapped up every moment of the European Tour, and then I should have been thanking my lucky stars that I was on the PGA Tour, but I couldn't see it like that. Ever since The Open, ever since the world had gone all mad and everyone wanted a bit of me, just being there wasn't enough. In 2016, it was all a great big adventure and I was just happy to be there. By 2017, I wanted more.

As I said earlier, the big problem was that my level of fame was completely out of line with my level of performance. People were treating me like a legend, but I hadn't done anything to deserve it. I was embarrassed by it. I was trying to force myself to catch up with the legends so that it would all even out. I was trying to force myself to get much, much better. And you can't force golf.

The media attention was insane. There's that survey saying people are more excited about seeing me on the PGA Tour than Tiger Woods, that blew my mind. I went to Los Angeles and I got invited on the Chelsea Handler show. I went to New York and I got taken on a tour of the city's best burgers. I didn't feel like I deserved any of it. But I desperately, desperately wanted to get to the part where I did.

The way I saw it, if I'd finished in the top ten of a Major, then I should be able to win a Major. And there's nothing wrong with that, is there? You have to believe in yourself, don't you? Anything else would be defeatist. If you don't believe you can win, then there's no point playing. So I wanted to hit that level of peak performance every single time I picked up a club. But there's a fine line between a healthy level of belief and utterly unrealistic expectations, and I had just screamed over that line at about Mach 3.

It was all so stupid. I wasn't even doing badly. In fact, I was doing pretty well given how quickly I'd risen up the ranks. But try telling me that. In 2017, I finished tied for 27th at The Open at Birkdale. A couple of years ago, I'd have been over the moon just to play there. Now I was fucking fuming because I didn't win it. And that was the day after I'd had that very public run-in with a radio station on Twitter. Again, the signs were all there if anyone had been looking for them. A mid-20s finish at The Open? I should have been delighted, that's a great week.

What I should have done was look back at the week with a clear head. I should have identified a couple of things to work on, aspired to hit a few more fairways or sink a few more putts. I didn't need to rebuild my game or anything. This is a sport of impossibly thin margins. A couple of tweaks, a slight improvement and all of a sudden I'm pushing for those top-ten finishes I wanted.

But I couldn't see it like that. I saw it as another failure. And so the next time I went out, I pushed myself even harder. And we all know how that goes on a golf course.

Unrealistic expectations ruin everything. They overtook my brain. I'd hit one onto the green, 20 feet from the hole. A perfectly fine shot. But I'd be all, 'Argh! For fuck's sake!'

A good putt, the ball rolls around the lip of the hole, I tap in for the par. For fuck's sake!

I should have been fine with these shots, but they just made me fume at myself. I was like that all the time. And it just carried on getting worse and worse.

It wasn't a constant thing. I was fine when I was in my hotel room. I could just shut the door and be alone. No-one could come in and I just had peace and quiet. But eventually I'd have to go back onto the golf course, and that's when the anxiety grew. In 2017, I was able to brush it off and sleep. By 2018, I was struggling to do that. I'd just stare at the ceiling wondering what the fuck was going on.

Knowing deep down that it wasn't going to get any better the next morning.

Amazingly, it was around this time that I met my wife, Jodie. She must have caught me on a good day. But I was hanging on by this point. She was travelling with me at the end of the 2018 season. I played in Hong Kong and I was horrible. I only missed the cut by a couple of shots, but I was really, really horrible. I wasn't in the right head space at all. I got myself to Australia for the next tournament but things just weren't improving.

I was playing with Cam Smith, I played a couple of holes and it was awful. I got this feeling inside me, this rising sense of fear. I just wanted to run away, straight off the golf course and away. I just wanted to get away from the people. Jodie was there with our group and I turned to her and said, 'Fuck this, I need to get out.' I'd just had enough, I needed to run.

She said, 'What on earth are you talking about? You're in the middle of a game, you can't just walk off!' She talked me down, kept me calm and I finished the round and got through the week. But that was a massive red flag. That was the first time I'd got myself in such a state that I was prepared to walk off the golf course. That was the moment I thought, 'Oh shit, that's not good.'

Jodie wanted to talk about it afterwards, of course. She was worried about me, she had a lot of questions, but I just wanted to bat them away. I told her I didn't want to discuss it and that I just wanted to go out for dinner. Have some drinks, have some food, forget about it all. It was like a sticking plaster on a gunshot wound. But there was always another tournament looming up ahead.

I spent all Christmas, when I should have been relaxing and recharging my batteries, dreading the next one. I didn't want to go to Abu Dhabi at all. Couldn't think of anything worse. I went, though, played horrible again, obviously. I told my caddie, 'Mate, if you get the offer of another bag, you should take it. Promise me you'll take it because I don't know what the fuck I'm going to do next.'

I didn't want to have anyone relying on me. Caddies have got to earn a wage, they need their bonuses. If I'm playing shit, if my head's not there, I'm basically useless. I pushed him away, he went and found another player and when we went to Dubai for the next one, Jodie was my caddie. The fewer people I had who relied on me, the better.

Looking back now, it's all so obvious. I was trying to make it easier to walk off the golf course the next time. I was deliberately clearing the obstacles to make it easier to run away.

And yet it didn't happen in Dubai. Something else happened. Me and Jodie had a laugh out there. It was all okay. I played the back nine really well on the Friday, made the cut, hit a decent score on the Saturday, finished tied for 24th. Problem solved, right?

Wrong.

We went out to Australia and again, the first day went really well. I shot a 66, one of the better scores of the day. Couldn't have been easier. And then the next day I woke up and it was like a thick mist had come down over me. I've never known anything like it. You know when people say that they can't think straight? This is exactly what that was. It was a total brain fog. I couldn't do simple things. I couldn't write numbers in my yardage book. I'd write the wrong ones, or I'd write them backwards. And that was before I even swung a club.

I couldn't get my head around it. One day I'm shooting six under, cruising round the course. Then the next day is a disaster. I was on a different planet that day, I was on those fairways in body only.

Mistakes were coming out all over the place, it was like I'd never played a competition before. On an straightforward course, with everyone else getting 60s, I hit a 77 and missed the cut. I'd been so happy for the first time in so long and then it was right back to square one, but with the added embarrassment that I seemed to have forgotten how to count or write numbers. I walked off the golf course at the end and I felt this sense of relief. Thank fuck I didn't have to stick around for another two days of that. No professional golfer should ever miss the cut and walk off thinking like that.

Jodie and I went to Melbourne for a few days and had a blast. I just forgot all about the golf and focused on her and having an amazing weekend. And then it was all over and all I could think was, 'Oh fuck, when's the next tournament? I can't do another tournament.'

'What the fuck am I going to do?'

When I was young, I used to play football in the street outside my house. We had this next-door neighbour, she was always really angry and she hated kids who played football. You know the type; one of those old ladies who keeps your football if it goes in her garden. Well, me and a mate are having a kick-about in the street, he just chips the ball up to me and it sits up so perfect. You know how it is, when the ball just sort of hovers in front of you and begs to get spanked. So I gave it what it wanted; I absolutely twatted it and it streaked off like a missile, straight through her front window.

And you know that horrible feeling that follows a moment like that? That icy cold sweat, that thing you get when you just want to run away in any direction? That's how I felt whenever I thought about golf. And it was getting worse and worse.

It's astonishing that I lasted so long before the inevitable happened. We went to Perth for a tournament and they were so good to us. They really looked after us. I felt an obligation to perform, that pressure to really show up. We were at the practice day, a pro-am day, when the feeling hit me like a tidal wave, and I turned to Jodie and said, 'I can't do it.'

She tried to talk me down again, but it wasn't happening this time. Not a chance. I was like, 'I'm done, I'm out. I can't do it.' I let everyone down, all those people who wanted to see me play, the people who'd looked after us. I felt awful. I just went back to the hotel room and cried my eyes out.

Jodie was amazing. We hadn't even been together that long at the time. We weren't together before I suddenly got famous, we weren't together for the fun bit when it was all TV shows and free stuff. She just got this bit of me. It must have been such a shock for her, but she was so incredible and supportive.

We went home, I took some time off and planned to come back for the Indian Open, but at the last minute I pulled out again. I couldn't do it. And that's when Jodie turned around and said, 'You need to see someone. You need to get real help.'

I was pretty resistant at first. I said no, I was really stubborn about it. I found the whole idea of asking for help to be really embarrassing. I didn't want it to be a big thing.

But it *was* a big thing and eventually I gave in and went to see one of the sports psychiatrist Steve Peters's people.

It took me a few sessions to get into it. I wasn't comfortable with it at first, but soon I was able to open up and explain how I was feeling. I just said to them, 'I literally don't know what's going on in my head. I can't physically get myself onto a golf course.'

But they started to break things down and we were able to talk about how quickly everything had happened, how quickly the fame had come around and how unprepared I was for everything. And I found myself thinking, 'Fucking hell, you're right. That makes sense.' I'd never even thought about it before.

That was the first stage, understanding the problem. The second stage was finding a way to cope with the problem. And really, it's just like practising your golf. You're just practising your mental side. You're practising how to deal with what's in your head. Things like allowing yourself to fall short every now and then.

Realising that golf is a game where you're going to lose way more than you're going to win.

There's such a fine line between belief and expectation. And if you cross over from belief to expectation, it can get dangerous. And that's what I did. I crossed over, I expected to win, I piled pressure on myself to win and then I was furious with myself when I didn't. And I did it for two years until it all got too much. I can see it now, but I couldn't then. Now I can train my brain to see where the line is and stop short of it.

I can say, 'I might win ten tournaments, but I might not win one.' Am I going to *try* to win ten tournaments? Yes! Fucking hell, yes, I am. But if I don't, it doesn't matter. My mind was blown at how simple it all was when you put it like that. And I couldn't believe how simple it was to fall off and slide down a slippery slope out of nowhere.

Those days where I was most angry with myself, they weren't even bad days. I was only a few years on from those little Jamega events and suddenly I was on the fucking PGA Tour missing the cut by a couple of shots. I would have killed for that, I would have grabbed it with both hands if you'd offered it to me back in 2011.

And the weird thing was that when I first got my European Tour card, I was terrible. I had a fucking horrible year in terms of performances, but I didn't bat an eyelid. Back then, I just thought, 'It's okay, it's my first year, I'll just go back to the Challenge Tour and go again.' I could shoot ten over and be fine about it. But I lost that mindset after The Open in 2016.

It wasn't Valderrama that did it to me, it was The Open. Finishing in the top ten in a Major against one of arguably the best fields of the year, the best players in the world. That was what sent me astray.

If my golfing career was a graph and there were two lines, one for my performance and one for my popularity, that was where it went wrong. My performance line was going up nice and steady and then my popularity went vertical, straight up in the air, and I couldn't handle it. I tried to force the performance line to meet it and I lost all perspective.

I didn't know what was going on or why everyone wanted a piece of me. Was it just because I had a big beard? Is that why people wanted to have their picture taken with me? What the fuck was it about me that was different? I felt like a fraud. They were treating me like a legend and I wasn't one. I didn't want to be a clown who was known for playing bad golf and messing around. I didn't want to fail.

Back in 2012, I could fail on the European Tour and no-one would really notice. But now there were other people's expectations to contend with. People knew who I was, or to be more accurate, they had their perception of who I was. I used to really worry about that. I wanted to live up to what they thought about me, not fall short. I'd walk onto the course thinking, 'You've got to play well today, people are watching you. If you play shit, you're going to look like an idiot.'

One of things I've learned from the psychology is that if you take five people and ask them about another person, by and large, one of the five will really love that person whatever they do, three will make a judgement according to what they see, and one will really hate that person whatever they do. So the doc says, 'On that basis, how many people do you think hate you already before you've even done anything? So why are you bothered by what people think? Some people will hate you whatever you do.'

In the past, I'd worry too much about what people thought of me. I felt like there was a target on my back. People are watching you, they're watching your scores. They want to talk about you, they want to spread shit about you. And now I know that you just have to let them. It's out of your control.

So after getting through all of that, it was a question of, 'Can I do this again? Can I get back out on the golf course and do all of this again? Can I get in the right frame of mind?'

It was 2019, I'd missed several months of the season, I've got four months to try to keep my tour card. Am I up to the challenge? One hundred per cent, I felt that I was.

Golf is hard and if you have one bad season, you can effectively lose your job. You can wind up back on the Challenge Tour and never make it back to the big time. So that fear hangs over you all the time. But even with that, even with what I'd been through, even though the challenge was tough, I was now absolutely certain that I'd be okay.

I felt fucking nervous coming back. In that first tournament I'd put it into my head that I didn't need to make the cut. It wouldn't be a disaster if I didn't make the cut. What I needed to do was simply prove that I could get out on the golf course and play again. That I could cope with a bad shot without wanting to run away and hide. But I did that and I did a bit more. I actually made the cut and I felt like I'd played well.

Then I made the cut in the German Open too. And then I was tied for fourth in the Scottish Open. And I felt different. I felt, and I don't want this to sound bad or disrespectful, but I felt like I didn't give a fuck anymore. In a good way. I felt like I had a different mindset now. That I could go around the course, that people could say what they wanted, that the tension could rise and I'd be okay. I was just playing golf. Playing golf for myself, not for anyone else's expectations. I felt like I had new wiring.

I could handle my emotions better now. I could deal with a bad shot and brush it off. I was doing everything they told me to do. And that performance in Scotland got me back in The Open, back into the fire again, back to the tournament that meant the most to me.

I missed the cut by a couple of shots but instead of being furious at myself, I was really pleased with the way I'd handled the week. I was playing the best sustained period of golf of my career. But this was no longer the most important thing in my life. I was about to become a father.

Jodie was pregnant. Because we travelled together around the world, we didn't really have a home base. We didn't have a local GP and we didn't even know which hospital we were going to be in for the birth. My performances since I'd been back had been enough to put me in contention for the really lucrative, reduced-field tournaments at the end of the year, but I turned them all down. There was only one place I wanted to be and that was by Jodie's side for the birth of my child.

Harley was born safe and sound in November 2019, and I was happy to step away from golf and be there for her and Jodie. You could line me up for any tournament, any prize money, and my family would always come first. Besides, there was always the 2020 season, wasn't there? I was back, I was better than ever, I was a father and I had the rest of my career to look forward to. Just in time for the world to change.

I remember going in to see the doctor about a shoulder problem in early 2020 and they had the news on in the waiting room. The first case of Covid had just been discovered in the UK and even the doctor looked worried. 'We're in for a rough ride here,' he said.

I didn't really understand it. I thought it was just going to be like SARS or swine flu. How rough could it be? And then we all found out together.

It was frustrating to be stuck in the house just as I was getting back into my stride, but I was counting my blessings. Some people had to give birth in the lockdown; we'd had Harley a couple of months before. Some people were stranded in different parts of the world; Jodie, Harley and I were together. And I can't imagine what it would have been like had I not spoken to someone in 2019 about my mental health. Taking that unresolved anger into a full lockdown could have been disastrous. Compared with some people and compared with how it might have been, we were quite fortunate.

When the 2021 season started up again, it was very difficult. Jodie and I were used to travelling together, we wanted to get back out there as a family, but we weren't allowed. I didn't want to leave them alone and it drove me nuts.

I could never quite get a rhythm going that year. Partly through the travel problems, partly because of the nagging shoulder injury, and then it really didn't help when I apparently came into contact with someone who had Covid and I got pinged. That got me locked in a hotel room for ten days while the Middle East events were kicking off.

All of a sudden, I found myself having to play to keep my card again. I needed to get some results on the board or I was going to get knocked off the European Tour. And it's in this period that I'm being asked to get the Covid vaccine.

Now I've got no problem with the vaccine – it brought us all out of lockdown and it saved millions of lives – but I was reluctant to get it for myself. Partly because I was young and healthy and didn't think I was at risk, but also because I'd heard that it made your arms ache. I already had a shoulder problem and I really needed to play golf. But the Tour was pretty insistent about it and I wasn't able to travel for events if I didn't get it.

I was going back and forth on it for ages, but there I was in a taxi heading for a cortisone injection on my shoulder and I thought, 'Right, time to just get it done and move on.' So I asked the driver to swing by this centre where I could jabbed. I jumped out, got the injection and got back in the cab for the doctors. When I got there, I told them that it was all cool, I'd got myself vaccinated.

'Oh,' they said. 'That means we can't give you the cortisone. You'll have to wait two weeks before you can get it now.'

So that was me out of action for even longer! I was out of the running for the Race to Dubai, with only a few events left in the year. The pressure was back on.

But I did have a new coach, Jamie Gough, and he was really helping me to refine my game. He kept things very simple, he avoided complications and I started to play really well. I went to Wentworth for the BMW PGA and only missed out on the win by three shots. I ended up finishing sixth, which was brilliant, but the margins were so fine. It could have been even better. As it was, it was enough to pretty much guarantee the retention of my tour card. I played a few more events, and as 2021 drew to a close I was mentally drained, but satisfied that I'd made some big steps forward.

I had a vision of where I could be now. My target for 2022 was to make the Ryder Cup team. I felt that was a realistic goal. I was in the best shape of my life. I had a good rest at Christmas, recharged the batteries and I felt more than capable of coping with a new season. In terms of performance, I was gaining consistency.

Wentworth was further proof that I could compete at the top, but I was no longer unable to handle my emotions if I found myself further down the leaderboard. Six years on from that breakthrough season, I felt mature, stable and happy.

And that's when I got injured.

I was warming up one morning in early 2022 and my thumb felt strange. It wasn't painful at first, just a bit weird. And then I hit a shot and it went pop and I thought, 'What the fuck was that?'

I came off the golf course and I was really worried. It didn't feel right at all. I got an injection and hoped it would go away, but it didn't. No-one seemed to know what it was. The first doctor I saw told me to take a load of painkillers and see if it sorted itself out.

I was like, 'Are you fucking kidding me? I can't even make a back swing, I don't think painkillers are going to help.'

The next doctor laughed at the first doctor's painkiller idea. What a terrible doctor, he said. Then three months later, he was out of ideas. He didn't have a clue what it was. 'Take a load of painkillers,' he said. That wasn't very helpful.

I said, 'You laughed when I told you that was what the other doctor said.'

He said, 'I just can't see anything on the scan. Maybe you should just give it four months' rest.'

I felt like I was getting messed around and I was scared. Your brain starts spinning out of control and you think, is this it? What if my hand is never right again? But what could I do? Just take their advice and hope it all worked out.

So I gave it four months' rest. That took me up to December and the start of the 2022 season. I started swinging a club again and I felt it was back to normal, so I went to Dubai for one of the first events of the season. For two days it was like I'd never been away. I made the cut after nearly a year on the sidelines and I felt great. And then on the third day it blew up again and I was in agony. I wasn't going to back down, though. I'd made the cut, I hadn't played for a year, so I took the advice of those doctors and necked a load of painkillers. By the final day I could barely feel a thing, but not in a good way. The hand was strapped and I was just getting myself around the golf course.

I saw a doctor in Singapore a couple of weeks later and what he said absolutely terrified me. I'd felt pretty good at first because he seemed to know what had happened. He'd seen the scans, he'd given me an MRI, they'd identified a swelling inside a bone in my hand, caused by me forcing myself round on painkillers.

He said, 'There's a 20 per cent chance that you'll never play tournament golf again.'

I said, 'Huh? I thought you said you could fix it?'

He said, 'We need to drill into the bone and inject calcium phosphate, a sort of liquid bone, in there to fix the problem. But there's no guarantee that it will be a good enough fix for you to play professional golf.'

But what can you do? I couldn't play golf the way I was, so I just had to roll the dice and hope it worked out. I went for the surgery. The anaesthetic was so strong that when I came round I got really confused and shouted at the nurse to stop slapping me around the face. No idea why. She wasn't anywhere near me. Whatever they give you, that stuff is strong. But I wish it had lasted longer because the pain after the surgery was something else. It took months to go away. And when it finally passed, I still had to see the hand therapist to get whatever the original problem was sorted out.

She diagnosed a problem in the tendon that runs from the top of your thumb all the way through your hand and down into your elbow. She told me to be patient with it and we did some sessions together to get some strength back. It got to the point where I could do some chipping on the range, but she warned me that recovery would be slow. She said that 85 per cent of the problem would go away quite quickly, but the other 15 per cent would take much longer.

'How much longer?' I asked. It was March 2023 and I'd missed the start of the season already.

'November,' she said. 'You'll be able to play again in November.'

I couldn't believe it. I'd targeted the Italian Open in May for my comeback and now I was being told that I wouldn't even make it back for the end of the season. I was in shock. Everything had been fine at the end of the 2021 season, then I'd missed 2022 and now I was going to miss 2023 as well. What the fuck?

That was a tough time. For a while, I started to wonder if I was ever going to get back at all. And if I couldn't play golf, what else was I going to do? If you can't play, you can't earn money. I've got a wife and daughter, and I can't provide for them if I can't swing a golf club.

I started thinking about alternative careers. Could I go into coaching? I did some teaching when I was in Singapore and I'd started to look at coaching jobs on the PGA website. Would I make it back in November? I just had no idea if what I was being told was even true.

But this doctor was so accurate. Like, really weirdly accurate. As I write this, it's the end of October and I'm ready to play again. I've been slowly bringing myself up to full speed, I'm hitting golf balls hard again and I'm preparing to go and play tournament golf. It took me a while, but I finally found a doctor who knew what they were talking about.

The European Tour have been really good to me as well. They understood that I couldn't play and I was given a medical exemption, so they've looked after me well. I'll start the 2024 season as normal and I've got the whole year to earn my card for 2025.

When I sit down with Jodie and talk about what we've been through it just seems incredible. It's almost like a fresh start. When she came into my life, I was ranked in the top 100, but I was coming apart at the seams. She was there for me, she guided me through it, she made me get help and we've made a family together. Now my world ranking is fucking miles off, but everything else is better. I'm starting again, but I'm a very different person now.

I feel like I can wear everything I've been through like a suit of armour, you know? That I've got the experience and the wisdom to get through anything now.

I don't know if I'll get back to where I was in 2016, challenging for a Major, but I do know that I'll be able to cope with everything that goes with it much better. The pressure isn't going to get to me, I'm not going to fight with my own expectations. I can handle it now.

Coming back into golf doesn't scare me. I used to get nervous before tournaments, but I don't get that now. I don't feel sick thinking about it. I know what to expect.

But I know that I wouldn't have got through this without Jodie. I wouldn't be playing golf now if it wasn't for her. She's the one who fights for me, she tells me off if I'm slipping back into bad habits. Without her, I'd be finished.

10
CLUB CULTURE

I know what most people think about golf clubs. They think they're stuffy old places filled with bank managers and accountants wearing silly trousers and telling cringey jokes. And you know what? In some cases, they're absolutely right.

There are still golf clubs out there that are stiff and unwelcoming, throwbacks to the bad old days where the focus is what you look like, not who you are. So what do you do with them? You don't go to them. If I'm not welcome somewhere because of how I look or what I've got on my feet, I'll just drive off. I won't even bother. I can't stand that shit.

I think I was lucky with North Mid. It's never been a stuffy place. There are builders there, cab drivers and working-class people. There are wealthy people too, everyone gets along. The minute you walk through the door, social status means nothing. I've been going there since I was a kid and the whole place is like an extended family.

Mind you, I still had to have an interview before they let me join. I was nine years old, squeezed into a suit and sat in the boardroom with my parents in front of all these posh twats. This was 25 years ago, by the way, it's not like that now. I don't think I said too much, to be honest. It was just the standard, 'Why do you want to be a member?' Why did they think I wanted to be a member? I wanted to play golf! I was nine years old, I wasn't joining up so I could further my political career.

When I look back now, it was just absolute bollocks. I just remember sitting there in the boardroom thinking, 'Let me out of this fucking suit so I can go hit some balls!'

But you wouldn't believe what happened after that. I did that interview, my parents must have said all the right things, I got the all-clear and they accepted me as a junior member. I walked away thinking, 'Wow, I've done it. I'm a member and I can play golf whenever I want.'

And then I went home, tried out a mate's roller blades, stacked it over a stone and broke my arm. Unbelievable. The very same day I signed forms, I ended up in casualty with a plaster cast on my arm and I couldn't do a thing for nearly three months. My dad couldn't believe it; that after jumping through all of those hoops, I'd gone and done it. My mum still laughs about it even now.

But yeah, North Mid has changed a lot over the years. It's much more open there now, it's one of the most inclusive golf clubs around. But there's been a lot of arguments to get it there.

They used to have a rule that you couldn't wear black socks. Seriously. What's that got to do with anything? If I was out there playing and I saw someone chipping in on the 13th hole with black socks on, would it ruin my day? Would I faint from the shock of it? What's that all about?

As I got older, I started to push back on all of that stuff. I'd have friends who'd want to come up and have a drink, and they were told they had to be smart. But we didn't want to be smart. And eventually we just decided to ignore it all and dress how we wanted. So I'd rock up in jeans and a T-shirt with a pair of trainers on, and after six months of telling me off they eventually gave up.

I just never got my head around how illogical it all was. If I was to play on a wet day in January in really expensive, really acceptable golf gear, I could come into the clubhouse caked in mud and sit down for a pint and sandwich. But if I came in wearing clean jeans and a nice T-shirt, I couldn't?

It's like those nightclubs where you can't get in wearing a pair of trainers, but you can come in a pair of steel toe-capped black work boots. If I was a bouncer, I'd rather be letting in a kid in a pair of trainers than someone who can smash my kneecap with one swing of his leg. It doesn't make any sense.

Eventually, North Mid relaxed the rules and now it feels just right. Most people still come in dressed up pretty smart, they're still wearing their nice stuff, but that's their choice. You don't get kicked out if you're dressed like you're on your way to B&Q.

There are some golf clubs that have gone for a split solution: they have places where you can wear what you want and places where you have to be smart. I guess that's fine, but I still don't get it. If I saw people in suits, I wouldn't worry myself about it. I wouldn't hold it against them, I'd still happily to chat to them at the bar. But at least it's something. At least it's not a weird old place hanging on to traditions laid down centuries ago even though no-one can remember why.

I think Covid changed a lot of people's views. It's almost as if the disease woke people up to the seriousness of the situation facing golf. The game was dying on its arse.

There's no golf club so posh that it can't go out of business. I don't want to be too morbid, but everyone gets older. It's not enough for fathers to just bring their sons to replenish the dwindling numbers, it's got to be more widespread than that. The stigma, the idea that it's a middle-class or an upper-class sport, it's got to be combatted.

Before the pandemic, people were starting to get a bit nervous as there were clubs opening up footgolf areas, where you kick footballs into oversized holes (I've never played, but it looks like fun), in an effort to get people through the doors.

But you don't need gimmicks, you just need nice, welcoming places. And when the lockdown lifted, so many new players came out of the woodwork, willing to give it a try. And you see that reflected, not just in what people are wearing, but what the big manufacturers are making.

In the old days, golf shoes were sort of like brown leather brogues with weird flappy bits across the laces. Now they look like five-a-side football trainers. Major outlets are selling golf tops that are basically just hoodies and you're starting to see professionals wearing them out on tour.

There are people who still like to dress a certain way when they play golf, and that's absolutely fine. If you want to turn up in a suit and tie or a pair of plus fours, that's nobody's business but your own. But most people just want to be comfortable and they don't want to get a bollocking for doing so.

That stuff still happens everywhere, though, and it's stupid. I've had friends getting themselves told off for wearing shoes in the wrong part of the building or having their hat on backwards and they've just been put off the sport completely. It's so self-defeating. You've got clubs in financial trouble all over the country and the people who are supposed to safeguard the game are going out of their way to put people off the sport.

It is difficult to get into golf. Lots of new players are really anxious about how they're supposed to behave at the club because they just don't know what the rules are. And even when you do know what the rules are, you're still going to make mistakes. Everyone makes mistakes. You might walk into the wrong room or tee your ball up in the wrong place and then suddenly you've got some prick shouting at you. It drives me nuts.

I was at a course once and a friend of mine got shouted at. He'd only just started playing, he's something like a 36 handicap, he's only just figured out which way round to hold a driver and he put his tee down in front of the markers. You're supposed to tee off either level with them or behind them, but it's hardly crime of the fucking century. All of a sudden, someone's come out of the clubhouse and started berating him. After that, he couldn't hit the ball in a straight line, his anxiety levels had gone through the roof. And it was all so unnecessary. Someone could have just had a quiet word, but at some golf clubs you get certain members who just love to tell people off.

Again, this is a sport that's not exactly easy to get into in the first place. And it hasn't exactly got the best track record when it comes to accessibility. Let's start with the cost of it.

Even the cheapest set of golf clubs is going to set you back about £150, so the sport is a long way from something like football, where all you need is an old ball and jumpers for goalposts. Then you've got to be able to afford to actually get on the golf course. It's a bit more pricey than your local five-a-side pitch.

And for some people, the gates of some clubs have been locked no matter how much money they had. I have never understood why women were kept out of golf for so long. No-one has ever been able to give me a reasonable explanation.

The Royal & Ancient Golf Club of St Andrews only relaxed its ban on women in 2014. Muirfield only backed down and let women join in 2017 after the club had been banned from hosting The Open. And up and down the country, even if women *were* allowed in, sometimes they were treated appallingly, even once at my own North Mid about ten years ago.

We had a new member there and she was good. She was playing off a seven handicap, she could hit the ball miles and she was playing one day off the men's tees. And someone's come out of the clubhouse and told her off. A member of my golf club has actually stopped what they're doing, come outside and told her off for playing on the men's tees, even though she was better than 90 per cent of the men there.

That's one of the only times I've been furious with my club, I was so pissed off. Golf is for everyone. Doesn't matter what colour you are, what religion you are, how you identify, it's a game for everyone. I spoke to the club, I said I hope you're going to suspend him. When we've been naughty at the club, and as you'll read here, me and my mates have been pretty fucking naughty, we've been told off, we've been sent letters, the risk of the suspension has always been there. I said, 'I fucking hope you're going to suspend him because this is *way* worse.'

The woman in question never played there again and I don't blame her. So we lost a good player and for what? I can't stand the idea of segregation in a golf club. It doesn't even make any sense. You'll get some women who can comfortably outdrive men. You'll get some men who would probably be better off going from the women's tees. In fact, they should scrap the whole idea of men's and women's tees. It doesn't matter. It's not the fucking Ryder

Cup. As long as everyone you're playing with is fine with it, you should be able to tee off wherever you want to tee off.

The sport has got a lot better over the years, but there's still a long way to go. Fortunately, that was a one-off at my place. More often than not, there's a different kind of trouble. The kind that frequently involved me.

I was really lucky when I joined. I was young, but there was a good bunch of junior players there and they took me under their wing. They were all about four or five years older, but they looked after me and they're all still my mates today. It would have been easy for them to get rid of me, or ignore me or even just bully me, but they were always there and so it never felt intimidating for me. And you needed to have your mates there because there are some big characters in a golf club.

We had this one fella there, Dave Walsh, and I've never known anything like him. He was a great guy, he'd always help out the juniors, he supported the club, he was really popular. But after a few beers, he was a wild man. An absolute wild man. One of his favourite tricks was to drive straight onto the 18th green, which wouldn't be a notable achievement except for the fact that he was teeing off from inside the clubhouse.

You'd see him do it. He'd prop up the bar, get himself ten pints deep then open the back door, throw a couple of balls on the floor and start swinging. Once he had a practice swing in there with a wood, pulled the club back, hit the metal shutters above the bar and made the loudest fucking noise you've ever heard. We're all in tears, rolling about on the floor and he's, like, 'Yeah, this isn't going to work,' and he walks out.

But then he comes back in with a fucking drill and drills a hole in the floor so he can put a tee in and hit it properly! You've never seen anything like it. He got a few letters from the club …

Even when he went too far, he'd always make up for it afterwards. There was this mixed competition once and this poor woman was playing on the 18th and she just kept putting her shot in the water. Five times she managed it and Dave was standing on a table on the terrace shouting, 'No more! No more!' and laughing his head off, but then I think he realised he probably wasn't helping, so he ran off to the pro shop and bought a set of a dozen new balls to present her with when she came into the clubhouse.

There was another time when one of the members had broken her arm, someone famous had signed her cast and she'd decided that she was going to auction it off and give the money to the junior members' fund. It was a really lovely idea, the sort of generous act of consideration that you often get at golf clubs like North Mid, but it did have one major flaw: who on earth wanted to buy a stinky old plaster cast? Not Dave, certainly. He'd put away a load of pints and concluded that the best thing to do was pull it off the bar, jump on it, stick it in the bin and set light to it. The smell of that plaster going up in flames nearly caused the clubhouse to be evacuated.

This poor woman was so upset, she was just trying to be nice, but then Dave gave her £100 and said that he'd bought it, given it a good send-off and now she had her donation for the fund. He was always doing stuff like that, he was always in trouble, always getting letters. But everyone loved him and I was really saddened to hear that he'd passed away a couple of years ago.

My mate Ben O'Sullivan eventually became the head greenkeeper at North Mid and he could go one better than Dave. He could hit the ball onto the 18th green from the car park, straight over the clubhouse itself. Well … most of the time.

After a long session, we'd put bets on whether he could do it. Could he get a par from the car park? We've got video evidence of it. There's Ben, six pints in, wobbling in the night air and then just unleashing one into the dark sky. Or, just as frequently, into the window. And every time, we'd all put our hands in our pocket and paid for the damage. The local glazier must have loved us. I reckon the club gave Ben the job there just to stop him putting the windows in on a Saturday night.

The only drawback to growing up in a golf club is that everyone there knows exactly how old you are, so as my mates got older, they ended up drifting into the bar and I couldn't go with them for a pint. I had absolutely zero chance of getting served in there. It was the most frustrating thing in the world to see them growing up, thinking that it would be forever until I joined them. I made up for lost time on the night of my 18th birthday, though. I made up for so much time that the bar staff there wouldn't speak to me for a few days afterwards. Projectile vomiting is not a victimless crime.

Seriously, I didn't even know what I'd done. I came in a couple of days later and was met with an extremely angry barman. It turned out that I'd been doing some sort of shot competition, sambuca not golf balls, and I'd chucked up my guts in the urinals. I could only blush like a tomato and frantically apologise, even though I had no memory of it whatsoever.

That's when the real madness started. Late nights, too many drinks, stripping off and trying to swim across the pond on the 18th while everyone else fires golf balls at you. The best times of my life.

And when you're at a really good golf club, you just make friends with people you might never ordinarily meet. North Mid is full of people from different walks of life, all mingling through their love of their game. You can play with anyone, it doesn't matter how old you are or how big your house is. People just get on with each other.

Even when I was a junior, I could be out there playing with another junior, or someone in their thirties, or even someone in their seventies. Tell me one other sport where you can do that. There's no other place for me like it. It's a very special golf club with very special people.

That's why there's no other place I'd have wanted to be when I won that first tournament in Spain. It was the strangest thing. I won the trophy, spent two hours talking to all the media and then I was just sat there in the locker room thinking about North Mid.

I turned on my phone and I had all these messages from my friends, videos of them celebrating in the bar when they knew that I'd win, 40 or 50 of them, going crazy. That was just insane and all I wanted to do was to be back there, celebrating with them. It was such a powerful moment. I could remember being that little nine-year-old in a suit, being the kid on his own, being the kid getting looked after by the other juniors, all the scrapes and the chaos.

So I went straight from all those videos to the airline websites, desperately scrolling around, trying to see if I could get back that night. It wasn't to be, but when I did eventually make it, the celebrations were so good they ended up on the *Daily Mail* website.

It's weird. Everything changes and nothing changes. The club is more open, more accessible, more friendly and yet it doesn't really change at all. When I go back there, it's the same old faces, people I've known for 25 years, people I can just sit down and have a chat with. It's a very special kind of environment.

Sometimes I like to imagine the sort of golf club that I'd run, and maybe it's something I'll do when I finally hang up my clubs and retire. I can see myself doing that.

The first thing I'd do is get rid of men's and women's tees, there's no room for that sort of bollocks at my club. We'd play all the proper rules for competitions, obviously, but when you're just there for fun, you can tee off wherever you like.

And there's obviously no dress code either. Come as you are. The only rule at my club is there are no rules.

I'd have a little pitch and putt area too – I want a place where people who have never even held a golf club can get involved and that means a little crazy golf course too. You can never have too many fibreglass dinosaurs in my opinion. That gives you a little career path as well. You can play the crazy golf course when you're a toddler with a little plastic club. If you like that, you can work your way up to the pitch and putt, and if you're still having fun and you want to continue you can come and join my club when you think you're ready. I won't even make you wear a suit and question you about your motives.

And I'd want a good bar. There's got to be a good pint of Guinness. That's one of many reasons I love playing at Druids Glen. But if I've got Guinness in my club, I'd want to try to get it as good as they have it in Ireland. I've never understood how they make it so much creamier and heavier. Everyone says it's the water, but that just sounds mad. Surely that's a problem that can be fixed?

I've got high standards for that sort of thing. There's nothing as disappointing as shit Guinness. You know, when it's got a mottled, yellow top, like the ceiling of a pub that hasn't been painted since the 1970s? There'd be none of that at Club Beef.

We'd have lots of craft ales too, I love them. There's so much good stuff out there now. I've been drinking this stuff called Lost Lager by BrewDog recently, it's amazing. We'll have a tap of that on the bar.

For me, that's for strictly after the golf. I know some people can have a few pints and play a decent round and I know this will make me sound uncool, but I cannot play at all if I've got alcohol in my system. I don't know how people do it, even a single pint ruins me.

And while we'll still have a clubhouse for the members, I want one for everyone too. I want people to come along, eat good food, drink good drinks, play board games, watch live sport and look out of the window at my golf course and think … maybe I should give this sport a try.

Food-wise, I'm taking full control. If it's the summer, I'm going to be out in the car park smoking meat. My wife and I just landed a job at *BBQ* magazine as roving reviewers and, outside of playing golf for a living, it's the best job in the world! So I'm going to be out there making brisket, while someone else will have to watch the bar on those days.

But the most important meal in a golf club is, of course, the club sandwich. You can't mess about, you can't cut corners, you need the best ingredients. So that's good, toasted white bread and grilled chicken breast for starters. Then you want crisp lettuce, not old flimsy stuff. You want firm tomatoes, cut thinly so that you don't drag them out of the sandwich and over your lap because you haven't bitten through the skin properly. And bacon. You need really good bacon. A squirt of mayonnaise and you're in heaven. I know some people put cheese in it too, and I'd have that as an option, but that feels like overdoing it. Either way, it's got to come out with a toothpick through the middle or it's not the real thing. It doesn't count if it hasn't got a toothpick.

We had that Natalie Coleman off *MasterChef* for a while at North Mid. She made this fish finger sandwich and it was one of the best things I've ever tasted in my life. She'll be head chef for me. She had a lot in her locker: proper Scotch eggs, sausage rolls, pork pies. You wouldn't go hungry at Club Beef.

And in the mornings, it's all about the breakfast buffet. Is there anything in this world that lifts the heart more than a row of those metal trays filled with bacon, eggs, sausages, mushrooms, the whole works?

Oh, and if you've come for the day and you've eaten well and drunk too well, we'll also have a few spare rooms so that you can crash over. I mean, on those nights when you've overindulged and you're wobbling at the bar worrying about getting a cab and not being sick on the seats, how much would you happily pay to take yourself out of the equation? We'd provide that service quite happily, not least because I might need it myself every now and then. We'll always have you covered.

I asked my publishers if I could say that I would have a very liberal attitude to licensing laws and that I'd do lock-ins, but apparently it's not a good idea to incite people to break the law in print, so I want to be *absolutely* clear that I wouldn't have lock-ins at all at Club Beef. I certainly wouldn't have really heavy curtains that block the light and make it appear from the outside that everyone's gone home even if they're all in the bar and I've made the jukebox and the pool table free to use and someone's just suggested shots …

The more I talk about it, the more I want to do it. No bollocks, no rules, no 'women can't do this' or 'women can't do that'. My golf club is about the golf, the drinks and the food. The food is key, man. The food is key.

11

APPROACHING THE GREEN

If teeing off is the most spectacular part of the game and putting is the most dramatic, then the big bit in between, the approach, is definitely the most strategic. This is where the sport becomes the perfect blend of mental strength and physical action. You need to know the course, know yourself and know how to put it all together to maximum effect.

But before we get into all that, I've really got to get this off my chest: television can give you such a misleading perception of golfers. When you're watching on the TV, you generally only see the best players playing well, hitting their best shots. If the coverage cuts away to someone in 20th place, 100 yards off the green, you know they're going to drop it five feet from the pin, or even put it in, because otherwise why would the producers cut away?

Seriously, you can watch hours of golf and never see a bad shot. Some people must think we never hit a bad shot.

I wish that was the case. But golf is hard and it doesn't always go the way you want it to go.

Video games don't help either. I love the idea of *knowing* that you'll always hit the ball perfectly. And I really, really like the idea of *knowing* that you're 160 yards from the green, *knowing* that the wind is negligible, *knowing* that you've got a four iron that does 170 yards when you hit it right and *knowing* exactly how to give it 95 per cent and drop it down next to the pin. Oh, and if it goes up in the air and looks like it's going wide, how amazing would it be to just stick some sidespin on the ball while it's in midair? That sounds like a great sport!

The truth is that you only know roughly how far away from the pin your ball landed and it's mostly an estimate. You've got a little book for yardage and there are markers you can use to pace it out and get a sense of where you are, but that's as good as it gets.

The wind, I am sorry to tell you, doesn't blow consistently like a desk fan. It blows in gusts or it just doesn't blow and it certainly doesn't warn you in advance. You can't see how far your strength bar has filled up on your backswing and you can only ever try to feel your way to 95 per cent.

As for the length you can get with your clubs, it's down to you to learn that bit. You need to memorise how far you can hit a ball with each club. And finally, you have to remember that even professionals don't hit a perfect shot every time. Sometimes we don't even hit the ball properly. It's hard.

I couldn't tell you how many bad shots I've hit over the last 15 years. It's in the hundreds, it happens all the time. You step up and you think, this is easy enough, and then you miss the green.

Honestly, if you can hit half the greens you're aiming at from 100 to 120 yards out, you're doing just fine. I used to love playing Tiger Woods on the PlayStation when I was young, but the real thing is much, much harder. That's why it becomes an obsession for so many people.

There can be a lot of luck involved in golf too. Sometimes you can hit a near-perfect shot and end up in a bunker. Sometimes you can hit a poor shot, drift 30 yards off your line, but end up somewhere that's perfectly fine. An inferior shot might still put you in sight of the green when your friend who hit a great shot has ended up in someone else's divot on the fairway. You can hit the fairway where the grass is lovely and short, but you're on an awkward slope, or you can get a bit of rough that isn't actually that bad. And you have to be mentally prepared for that.

I always mentally expect the worst, so I spend that 300-yard walk from the tee thinking about my options. If you think you've hit the bunker, expect it to be in the bunker. So when you get there and it's not, it's an absolute bonus and you're in a good mood. It's much better to do it like that than spend the whole walk thinking, 'Please be okay, please be okay,' and then you get there to find it's really not okay at all. So tee off and then prepare yourself for being in the shit because it's always great when you discover that you're not.

I think I'm still traumatised from Wentworth. You know how I said that I came sixth, but it could have been so much more? God, it still hurts to talk about it now. The 18th is a par five and if you want to get into a great position on the fairway, you need to get over the corner of this patch of trees as it dog-legs from left to right. It's one of those risk-and-reward holes. You can play it safe and use irons, but if you go for it, you can get an eagle to finish. And I wanted an eagle.

It's Saturday and I'm playing well, so I take out the driver and get exactly the line I wanted. Too far left and you'll hit the bunkers, too far right, it's gone. And I've hit this one perfect. So I come round the corner looking for the ball and it's gone too far. It's hit the fairway, bounced hard and gone over the other side, down a slope and into heavy rough.

But I know I can do it now and so when I come to it again on the Sunday, the last hole of the tournament, I take out the three wood and hit the same shot, perfect line, straight over the corner of the trees. The first one was a driver, remember, it went too far. This should be just right.

I stride around the corner thinking, 'This is great! I've nailed it, how far now? It's going to be about 190 yards, I can do that with a six iron, I can make three, I can finish on an eagle!'

But as I come around the corner, I'm like, 'Where the fuck is my ball then?'

And you wouldn't believe it, but I've done the same thing again. Somehow a weaker club has given me exactly the same result, it's bounced off the fairway and away down the hill. And I know I've spoken a lot about trying to take things in my stride and not lose perspective, but that fucked me right off.

I finished sixth, three shots off first. So that's why it's a good thing to be mentally prepared for bad news. Especially when it actually *is* bad news.

The first thing you want to do after a bad tee shot is make it all better by doing something extraordinary. This is your ego kicking in because you feel hard done by and your brain is going, 'Fucking hell! That's not fair, it was a really good shot!' And you look at yourself, stuck in rough or in sand or behind a tree and you think, 'Maybe I can fix it … maybe I can still get to the green if I just absolutely smash it out of here. I deserve that.'

That's when you really need to take a moment. It's also where a good caddie can help you out. If I turn to a caddie and say, 'Oh come on, give me the six iron, I can get out of this,' I need them to say, 'What on earth are you think-ing?' and try to talk me out of it. It will still be my decision, but I'd like them to at least try to protect me from myself.

There have been so many times where I've done some-thing like that and, far from getting on the green, I've put myself in the water or something. I did it in Denmark once. Instantly, you're furious with yourself. 'You idiot! You absolute idiot. Why did you do that? There was no chance of you getting that. You're chasing a six now, you could have had four if you'd just been sensible.'

So you have to really control the ego and just do the sensible thing: get a pitching wedge, get yourself out of the shit and get back on the fairway. This is the mental battle you have to fight all the time, but especially when you think you've hit a good tee shot and you haven't been rewarded for it. Your brain kicks off and you push yourself too hard because it's a scoreable hole and you should be doing better.

For all that, I have to tell you about this one shot I saw from Alex Levy in Dubai. We were playing together. He was right on the cut line and he needed an eagle to make himself safe. He's on the last hole, a par five with a really difficult fairway to hit. We both ended up in the rough on the left. I walked up and saw a ball in deep, deep rough and I nearly burst into tears. 'Fucking hell! Is that my ball?' and someone said, 'No, your one is up there,' and I've never been so relieved in my life. It was still rough, but I was able to wedge it out and back onto the fairway easily enough.

I've turned around and Alex is pulling out a wood. I'm like, 'What the hell is he doing? He's got no chance, you can't play a wood in that sort of rough.' I would have bet against him every single time, but he took his wood, he took this big hard swing at it and not only did he get it out, he must have hit it 215 to 220 yards! I've never seen anything like it. Seriously, if that shot had been caught on camera, it would be racking up 20 million views on YouTube. Absolutely ridiculous. I do not recommend trying that on your local course. Far better to just take your medicine and get it back out on the fairway.

As I say, the most important part of improving everything in between teeing off and putting is to know your clubs and the limits of what you can do with them. There's a reason we're only allowed to carry 14 of them in our bag; it's because there's so much variety in what they can do, and the trouble they can get you out of in a tight spot.

So much is about the loft. Your wedges and your high irons are going to have open faces, so they sort of lift the ball up in the air. Something like a five iron will have more of a flat face, so that it smacks the ball hard for distance. As the numbers go down, so does the loft. And that's why you carry ten different irons. Drivers and woods, even more so. That's why Alex's shot was so extraordinary. If you hit rough or sand with an open-faced wedge, it gets underneath and almost digs the ball out and up into the air. Hit it with a flat face and it shouldn't go anywhere. I still don't know how he did it.

Sometimes it's worth choosing loft above distance, taking the more open club to get you out of trouble, rather than betting on the distance.

But distance is important too. When I'm playing with my friends what really stands out isn't their technique, or the way they strike the ball, it's the fact that they often haven't got a clue how far they can hit the ball with a certain club. I was over at Druids Glen in Ireland for a stag night recently and there's a green there with a big wall right behind it. My mate's stood up and hit this lovely shot, connected perfectly, and he's posing and celebrating as the ball soars right over the wall and away.

If you're going to get seriously better, you need to take your bag to the driving range and work on all of your clubs, not just your driver. Lots of them have got launch monitors now and you can use them to tell exactly how far you're hitting the ball. That's what I've done. You go through the whole bag and hit five or ten balls with each one, you note down the ones you hit perfectly, the ones you've absolutely flushed and then you can say, 'All right, I'm not going to hit it any further than that. So that's my number.'

But you also want to note the ones you don't get right and why you don't get them right. Have you tried too hard and got an extra five yards, but lost control? And what can you do if you take the power off just a little bit? Keep doing that, keep a record of the distances and you'll slowly develop something like that thing from the video games: the ability to say, 'It's 170 yards. I can hit a five iron 170 yards all day long.'

Then it's all about using that knowledge correctly. Most amateurs never consider the green. They'll think, 'The green is 150 yards away, I can do 150 yards with a seven iron,' and they won't notice that the green has got 20 yards behind the flag and bunkers in front of it. So they're okay if they hit it perfect, but how often does that happen?

Better to take the five iron and hit it and have much more chance of getting onto the back of the green and very little chance of ending up in the sand. Far better to take your next shot with your putter than your sand wedge.

This, again, is an ego thing. It's forcing yourself not to attack every hole like it's the last round at The Open. It's recognising that you'll almost never have the perfect alignment of distance required and distance generally achieved with the club. You have to play around, you're almost always stuck in between clubs.

But there's other stuff to consider as well. It wouldn't be golf if it was as easy as that. You have to consider the lie. Is the ball flat and easy to hit, do you have to account for that? There's the wind, is it going to have an effect on the distance you can hit?

And this is why this aspect of the game is so fascinating, because you're walking around with all of these numbers in your head and you're using them to calculate against the conditions.

There's different ways to use your wedges too. You need to be working those on the range too. Use your swing like a clock face. What can you do if you lift the club to 9 o'clock? What can you do from 10 o'clock?

They're some of the most important clubs because over a four-day tournament you could potentially have 20 to 25 wedge shots from 100 yards or so and you're trying to hit it inside 10 feet of the hole. Now if I've got 25 wedge shots and I hit them all within ten feet of the hole, that's a lot of birdie putt opportunities over 72 holes.

You'll see a lot of professionals who won't always go for the maximum distance because they're trying to get themselves to their favourite number. I like 100 yards, that's my preferred distance. Some players will never ever hit it 50 yards away from the green because they find that wedge shot more difficult. It's like footballers with free-kicks. They don't want to be too close because then they can't get it up and over the wall.

You can adjust your grip as well. I did it a couple of years ago because I didn't like trying to swing for a certain distance. It didn't feel natural. So I moved my grip right down and I just stayed there hitting shots where I could feel a really repeatable swing. I did it over and over again, and then I looked at the numbers. Suddenly I was getting them all within five feet.

So amateurs, just go and hit your wedges. If you can get comfortable with one or two different grips, all of a sudden it makes such a difference to hitting into greens and not worrying about being trapped on a distance you don't like. But it's all based on knowing exactly how far you can hit the ball. And that only comes with lots of practice.

And when you've done that preparation work, you'll be in a better position to select the right clubs in your bag. You'll find most pros will make little tweaks to what goes in their bag according to where they're playing or what the conditions are that day.

So if I'm going to go and play a links golf course and it could be quite a windy week, I'll put a two iron in the bag, something that'll hit hard and low and that won't go up in the air and end up on the wrong fairway. So I'll have a driver, a three wood, a two iron and then all the way down to my wedges. I'll have a pitching wedge, a gap wedge and a lob wedge, which is the club with most loft, usually about 59 or 60 degrees. That's my basic set-up.

If I'm playing a golf course that's wet with not much wind and there's a few par fives, I might put a five wood in the bag instead of the two iron, knowing that it's going to go higher and I'm going to be able to attack the par fives a bit better.

If there's a golf course where there's not much call for a two iron, I might swap it out for another wedge, just to tighten the gaps between the yardage I can make and to give me more options in getting onto the green.

Sometimes you can get even more technical and have your wedges altered specifically for the conditions. The angle between the leading edge of the club and the lowest part of the trailing edge is called the bounce. If we're getting spoiled and the trucks with all the fitters are in town, we might adjust that too. If you've got really firm, hard bunkers, you can take the bounce off and it'll help you break that compacted sand and maybe get you out of a triple bogey situation. We're fortunate enough in some tournaments to have a couple of days of practice rounds, and if the sand is firm or the grass is tight, we'll be in there going, 'Guys, can you build me a new wedge with a different bounce so I can play these bunkers?'

And yes, let's talk about those bunkers. Are they the things that all golfers fear? No. They're what most amateurs fear. That said, links bunkers are the hardest bunkers. They're so small and deep that they're the most penalising bunkers in all of golf. The bunkers at Royal

Liverpool for the 2023 Open would scare the shit out of anyone. They were some of the toughest that I've ever seen. They looked like something out of the First World War, piled up sandbags like a brick wall in front of your ball. But then you'd base your approach on that and manage your risks accordingly.

Tiger's won there without hitting in a single bunker, Brian Harman won in 2023 and only landed in two or three all week.

But most bunkers aren't that bad, and if you play them properly and you rely on your technique you'll be fine. The problem comes when you try to play a bunker shot with a square club face. That's the worst thing you can do because you'll just dig into the sand and you won't be able to get the ball out. You have to open up the face so it's almost facing the sky and you're hitting the sand an inch behind the ball. You get your weight distributed to the front foot to help that angle to come down on the sand, and you want to be cutting underneath it, like the blade of a knife.

We're lucky, we get to practice all the time and we spend time nearly every day hitting bunker shots, so we're used to it. In fact, there are occasions when you'd actually prefer to land in the bunker than the back of the green where you might run off down a slope. If you know you can get out easily enough, then it's just another wedge shot onto the green. This isn't the case on links golf courses, but if you're on a parkland course, you're on a par five and you hit into the front bunker on your second shot …

that's not the end of the world, that could be a good spot to get.

This is why golf is such an incredible game. There are so many variables, so many things that should make you stop and think about what you're doing. There's never an easy shot in golf. Even when you're a professional.

But you know what? Sometimes you can do the wrong thing and it actually works out for you. Sometimes things happen that you can never predict. I was playing Wentworth once, another dog-leg hole, and I've tried to shape the ball from right to left to make the corner and I've got it all wrong. I've put too much on it and it's heading towards a small group of spectators and out of bounds. I thought I was never getting that ball back, I thought I might have to play a provisional shot, just in case it was lost. But then I walked up there and this guy said, 'No, you're all right, it hit me and bounced back in.'

I was like, 'Oh shit, sorry!' And that's when you pull a glove out of the bag, sign it and hand it over with your heartfelt apologies and deepest gratitude. It cost me a bit of kit, but it saved me two shots!

12

THE RYDER CUP

Golf is a solo sport. Everything you do, you do for yourself. You might have a management group, or you might share a personal trainer with some other guys; that can happen with players as they come through the age groups in the USA. But generally, when you tee it up, you're only thinking about yourself, your life and your world rankings. Everything is me, me, me. And that's what makes the Ryder Cup so special. It's the only time when it suddenly becomes about another 11 players on your side, all fighting for the same thing. It changes everything. I absolutely love it.

You've got the greatest golfers from America facing off against the greatest golfers from Europe over three days of competition. The first two days are group events, foursomes and fourballs, and then it all comes down to a run of head-to-head matches on the Sunday. There are points up for grabs all the way and it's never over until it's over.

But it is a brutal way to play the game. As poor Scottie Scheffler discovered, there's absolutely no hiding place when it all goes wrong. Unlike football, where you've got 50 or 60 games in a season, you get three days and then that's it for two years.

I was in Rome in 2023 working for Sky Sports and the atmosphere at the first tee just blew my mind. Television doesn't do it justice.

It's the most insane thing I've ever seen, it's even bigger than the Majors. It feels like something special. So special, that I'm not ashamed to admit I got a bit teary as it all started off.

Golf tournaments can often be rowdy. As I've said, there are some places in the USA where it feels like you're playing at a stag party.

But it's a wide spread of rowdy. The support tends to be spread around various individuals and it's very rare that anyone is actively willing people to have a nightmare. The Ryder Cup is different, it's partisan. It's about backing your team and giving the opposition some serious stick. This one was the most partisan I've ever seen. I think about 90 per cent of the crowd were backing the Europeans and the Americans were wildly outnumbered.

It's not aggressive like a football match, it's more of a party vibe, but it can be pretty full-on. Nicolas Colsaerts was out there giving it the thunderclap with the crowd, there were songs for some of the players. It must be amazing when it's in your favour, but horrible when it's against you. I can totally see why the Americans tend to win in America and Europe do well in Europe.

The Americans will get their own back in two years when the Ryder Cup is held in New York. While the Europeans tend to be more tongue in cheek with their humour, the Americans can be much more direct and personal. I think a lot of the players get pretty wound up by it, especially when it's attacks on their wives or things like that. It's a bit more X-rated out there, a bit more rowdy.

The first Ryder Cup I remember watching was the infamous Brookline event in 1999. I'm not sure what was worse; the Americans' shirts or their attitude at the end. The match was all square, Justin Leonard had a 45-foot birdie putt, José María Olazábal had a 22-footer. Leonard put it away and the Americans went crazy, the players and their wives were dancing all over the green, celebrating before it was even over. It took ages for them to clear off and let José have a crack at halving the hole. And that was a lot of time to have to think about his shot. He missed it and they all went crazy again.

But you can understand why they were so excited. The Europeans only needed four points on the final day to win the tournament, so this was an incredible comeback. You have to make allowances for those sort of emotions and I think if you asked the Americans about it now, they'd be a bit embarrassed and regretful of the whole thing. It's all cool. Anyway, Europe got their own back at the Belfry the next time out …

The big story in 2023 wasn't quite that exciting. It was Patrick Cantlay's refusal to wear a sponsored hat, which was reported to be a response to the USA team's refusal to pay their players. That may not even have been true, but when the team is getting battered, everyone's looking for an angle. It made him come across as greedy and the crowd loved it.

Everywhere he went final day, the fans were jeering and waving their own hats in the air. And fair play to that dude, he birdied 16, 17 and 18 and won his game.

The fans are two or three yards away from him, thousands strong, and they're absolutely going for it. Imagine trying to do anything in those circumstances. You're trying to chip the ball onto the green, you're trying to putt, the adrenaline is coursing through your veins and then you've got everyone shouting at you. It's mad. To stand up in front of that sort of treatment on the final three holes of one of the most important rounds of golf he'll ever play in his life is incredible.

And then there was the Rory McIlroy row. Patrick holes brilliantly for birdie on the 18th and his caddie, Joe LaCava, one of the most experienced caddies in the business, starts waving his hat around in the air at the fans, a sarcastic response to the treatment that Cantlay's had all day. He loves this shit and he's walking all over the green waving that hat, even getting right up close to Rory as he's preparing to putt. Rory doesn't like that one bit, words are exchanged and the fans are all going off. Then later on there is a confrontation in the car park, and Rory has to be led away by Shane Lowry and put into his car. And it ends with Shane Lowry having to come onto the green to try to sort it all out.

Then later on there's a confrontation in the car park and Rory has to be led away and put into his car. It was amazing. You don't get that in any other golf tournament. They made up afterwards, sorted it all out with a text message, but this is one of the best players in the world and one of the most experienced caddies and they're kicking off. It's this tournament, it brings out the fire in people.

It's funny because generally most people on the tours get on with each other just fine. There's not really any big feuds, it's very rare that anything like that happens. Everyone knows how hard golf can be, everyone respects each other. But the Ryder Cup is an exception to that.

I haven't played in a Ryder Cup, but it's my ultimate ambition. The closest I've been to those sort of mechanics is on the amateur scene where I've played in boys tournaments in Europe. I was in Denmark once and it got very spicy with the home fans. I think I'd love it, I'd love the challenge of trying to silence the home crowd, I'd find it really funny to get booed for three days. I really want to be in New York in 2025, but not on the commentary team this time.

That's not to say that I wasn't honoured to be there with Sky. It felt really good just to be out on a golf course. After so long out you can sometimes forget who you are. I've had two years on the sidelines, and I've had moments where I think, 'Am I even a fucking golfer anymore?' And just to be in that environment again was really special.

People asked me if it was hard for me to be so close to it but not in it. I actually found it really helpful. I need to be in that environment, I need to remember what it's like. It was a good kick up the arse and a reminder of what I've been missing out on. But next time I want to be out there with a club in my hand.

To get on the team, you need to be performing. There are three selections based on world rankings, three more on European rankings and the six wildcard picks for the captain. The qualification points count from about a year and a half before the next tournament, so just in time for me to make my comeback. In the final six months, the points double as the teams try to ensure they're getting the form players.

Usually I prefer to focus on processes rather than targets, I'm not a big goal-orientated person, but this is the big thing for me now. But then it's still about the process, isn't it? If you're going to make the Ryder Cup team, you're going to be winning tournaments. You've got to be winning tournaments, it's that simple.

I'd love to get that call, to have the captain on the line telling me that I was one of his picks. That would be incredible. But the next few weeks waiting for it all to happen would be something else.

When I was doing the commentary, someone asked me how I'd feel out there on the first tee and, to be brutally honest, I just don't know. I think there's always going to be nerves regardless, but until you get there you've just got no idea. You can turn around and give it the big one, you can tell people that you'd relish a moment like that and you'd absolutely love it, but until the spotlight is on you, you've got no idea. There's nothing that can prepare you for that. I think you'd just have to get yourself into that headspace where you're really aggressive and strong, you just lean into the challenge. That's what I've been working on while I've been out, trying to channel that positive thinking, trying to amplify it until you feel unstoppable. But even then, I think you'd still be a little bit nervous.

The team aspect is the most fascinating bit, especially on the foursomes where you have to take turns with a single ball. If your team is tight and there's a good atmosphere, it's fine. There's a mentality with some teams. It's all, 'If you hit a bad shot, I don't want to hear you say sorry. We're a team.'

The Americans didn't build that spirit. I saw players shaking their heads in disappointment at their partners, but you can't have that. They were losing by a lot, they were getting properly beaten up on the golf course, but it's not the kind of attitude you want from your playing partner. You want someone who's going to be able to roll with the punches. Someone who gets put in the bunker by their partner but doesn't whine about it. It's not easy.

You also need to get the right balance of characters in your team. You can't have anyone who's going to turn to you and say, 'What the fuck was that?' You want some poker face in your partner.

You don't necessarily want the flair players or the distance drivers. You want people who hit a lot of fairways, who hit a lot of greens. The sort of players who don't make too many mistakes. Because this is not a forgiving format. Again, it's not like a Major where you've got four days of golf and there's room for the mistakes to hide.

But this is what makes it so awesome. In this format, the rewards for being bold are huge. You see players trying to pile the pressure on each other, making aggressive plays for the pin where they might otherwise just try to set it down somewhere close for an easy putt. So it becomes a balancing act. Do you take the risk of pushing harder and trying to unsettle your opponent? How do you react when he does it to you?

Jon Rahm did it on the 10th, he hit one of the most ridiculous shots I've ever seen at that level. He was in the rough down by a small wooden bridge and when I say that, I mean that the bridge was in his way. I've played this course, the green is really hard to hit even in normal circumstances, but with this bridge in the way, it should be impossible. Most people would take the hit, get the wedge out, knock themselves back into line and then get on with it. He's taken it on and somehow hit it up and around the bridge and onto the green. Incredible.

I know Luke Donald and he's very big on statistics in golf. He was captain in 2023 and he was working wonders with the numbers.

Who's best to pick in fourball, who's best for foursomes, all the little things that count when it comes to, not just getting the best line-up, but the best way to use your line-up. You want the right blend of characters, the right chemistry. You need to know when to play two leaders together and when to split them up to share the experience. The Europeans were very smart in the way they did this, pairing a seasoned Justin Rose with Bob MacIntyre in his first Ryder Cup – that was a genius move. He could lean on Justin, he could be looked after out there.

The captaincy issue is one of my favourite parts. When you go through the old tournaments, you find that the captains used to have a decent run of events. Tony Jacklin did 1983, 1985, 1987 and 1989. Bernard Gallagher did 1991, 1993 and 1995. These days, it changes every time and I kind of like that. It's become like a badge of honour, a sort of thank you for your service across multiple Ryder Cups. It keeps it fresh.

There's also a sense of progression there. You've got the rookies coming through and they're guided by the more experienced players. You've got the vice-captains picking up that leadership experience to set them up for when they take the big job. And then you've got the captain sitting above all of them, focusing on the big calls. It means that you'll never have a situation where someone comes in as the skipper but doesn't have a clue how to do the job.

I'm delighted that they've kept Luke Donald in place. He put so much into it, so many hours of preparation, and you can see how tight the team was under his leadership.

With that sort of team spirit anything is possible. My favourite Ryder Cup was the Miracle at Medinah in 2012. Europe were trailing 6–10 on the final day, the Americans only needed four and a half points to seal the deal and then Europe struck back. It was crazy, absolutely epic stuff. It's incredible that you can have two days where it feels like one-way traffic and yet it still turns around on the final Sunday. That's the beauty of the format, having 16 points available across the first two days and then 12 for the final day.

Literally anything can happen. And it's because it's so hard to win. When you look at the strength of both teams, there just aren't any weaknesses. Anyone can beat anyone in any game; it doesn't matter what the form book says or what the rankings are, Ryder Cup predictions are just a nightmare.

I think the beauty of the Ryder Cup is that it's a gateway for new fans of the sport. It sort of transcends the game of golf; the people who watch it, often they won't watch any other tournament in the year, they're just there for the clash between Europe and the USA. It's absolutely massive for the sport. Just look at the way it dominates the newspapers on the Monday morning.

But aside from the glory and the catastrophe, this is also a place for redemption stories. Let's go back to Scottie Scheffler. This is the world's number one golfer, and on the first day of the Ryder Cup he and his partner Brooks Koepka are absolutely destroyed by Viktor Hovland and Ludvig Åberg. They suffer a total historic humiliation and Scheffler breaks down in tears on the side of the golf course. My heart went out to him, it was absolutely brutal.

Not everyone knew at the time that he'd changed his putting coach a month before the tournament. I couldn't think of anything worse timed than that. It's hard to fight muscle memory and insert new techniques into your game at the best of times, but this must have been horrendous. I thought that was an absolutely crazy decision.

It must have been so difficult for him to stand up and feel comfortable playing golf in those circumstances. There's nothing worse than not feeling right on the green when everyone's watching you, especially when people are actively cheering every missed putt.

But he came back from that disastrous Friday. He went out again on the Sunday and he halved with Jon Rahm. And he did that after another bad start, missing a few short putts. That was pretty awesome. You have to understand the level of scrutiny. If you're in a Major and it's all going wrong, the television people will just stop showing footage of you and they'll focus on the people who are doing well. But this is the Ryder Cup. The cameras stay on. There's nowhere to hide. It's such a tough situation and any golfer would feel for him, but he really showed his class in coming back out fighting.

Look at Rory McIlroy. He was the one in tears in 2021 at Whistling Straits after a heavy defeat. Two years later, he was Europe's top points scorer.

And that's the Ryder Cup in a nutshell. It can break you, but it can remake you in a matter of hours, if you're strong enough. It's the biggest test of character, and I've got just under two years to earn the chance to go out and try it for myself.

13

FAMILY BALANCE

In any walk of life, maintaining a good work–life balance is key. Family is everything to me, and, no matter what I do with my life, I can never see myself as one of those people who prioritises their work above the people closest to them. You know what they say: 'No-one ever died wishing they'd spent more time in the office.'

I'm not judging anyone; what works for me might not work for other people and everyone's got their own way of coping, but I can't imagine leaving my family at home while I go around the world playing golf. I want them with me, I want us all to be going on the adventure. But even I couldn't have predicted that I'd have my wife caddying for me in a professional tournament.

It was at that time when I was in trouble and I was trying to get people away from me. I didn't want to drag anyone else down and I told my caddie to find himself something more secure than me.

And Jodie stepped up. We'd had a laugh about it in the past, but one day I just said to her, 'Why not?'

Finding her a bag was the hard bit. She's not the tallest girl in the world and she could probably fit inside one of my normal bags, so we had to get a little one for her. But she was amazing, she got right into it. And it was funny as well because some of those bunkers were really steep and she was having trouble getting in and out of them!

I think it worked for both of us. She felt like she could look after me a bit better and I had someone there with me who took the pressure off and stopped me from getting up inside my head.

But there is that thing, isn't there? About getting your wife to carry the heaviest bag? I felt really bad about it! I wouldn't make her carry the heaviest bags if we were coming out of Tesco, and this just didn't feel right. I was worried I was going to get cancelled for being mean to her. But no-one said anything. And, to be fair, it's not unheard of in the game. Lee Westwood's wife is his caddy. So it was weird, but it was okay.

In fact, it was better than okay. We were smashing it. The first two days at the Dubai Desert Classic in January 2019 were tricky, I wasn't quite on it, but then it clicked and I had a really good back nine on the Friday. I had a nice run of birdies across the last six holes and made the cut, so we were really happy. I got the putter going on the Saturday and we shot seven under, and for the first time in ages it was great fun.

She was really funny, sometimes unintentionally. She was still so new to golf, so she was really curious about it all. There would be moments where I'd hit it a bit off line or I'd miss the green and this voice beside me would go, 'What went wrong there then?'

I think if a normal caddie had done that, I'd chase them off the golf course, but she was just asking genuine questions, it was all innocent. And I don't know why, but it really settled me down. I had to try to explain myself and say, 'You know what? Sometimes you just play a bad shot, that's what I've done there, so let's crack on and hit the next one.'

Jodie was amazing. It was hard too. There are so many unwritten rules in golf, so much of the etiquette to learn, and she only had two days to learn it. It's silly stuff, like, if I hit the bunker then my caddy has to remember to go and rake it over later, to make it fair and keep the game moving. It's not a massive thing but if you don't do it, it can really upset people. So I'm going round the course, I'm working out my own yardages and I'm trying to stay on top of what she's doing too, reminding her when to take the flag out of the hole and stuff like that. It was a real crash course. I wasn't bothered about her making a mistake with me, of course. She was never going to piss me off. I was just worried that she might piss other people off.

Fortunately, we were playing with good people and the other caddies were really great with her. That's not a given either. Some caddies can feel pretty undervalued if someone else is carrying bags, and you can understand why. If you've got your wife or your mate carrying your bag, it's almost as if you're saying, 'Anyone can do this job,' and that's not true. But sometimes you need what you need.

Caddies *are* really important, they can play a huge part in someone's career. They're your right hand, they can get you out of trouble, they can help you focus and they can definitely prevent you from making silly mistakes. But sometimes as a player you can over-rely on them and I think I fell into that trap when I was struggling.

My position was that I didn't want to think. I didn't even want to carry the course planner that you get given at the start of a round. They've got all the yardages and the pin sheets in them, but I left that to them. But now I had to do it all myself. I'm pacing out the distances, I'm looking for markers to get a gauge on my position. I didn't have anyone there to help me, so I had to do it myself and it worked for me. I liked taking ownership, I liked having something to focus on. I couldn't ask Jodie if a six iron was going to carry the water or anything like that, so I had to think, 'Come on then, you know how to fucking play golf. Just do it.'

And if you're wondering whether or not we had any rows while we were out there, there was never any chance of that. I've never been one to get tetchy with Jodie, but to be honest, I'd never get tetchy with a caddie anyway. I've always had a very good relationship with them. I've seen it all out there with players blaming caddies for this, that and everything. I've heard players turn to their caddies and say, 'Oh yeah, left side of the pin, was it? Nice fucking call, dickhead,' and I'm thinking, 'You're the one hitting the shots, mate! There's no point taking it out on them!'

You can get the advice, you can get the experience, but at the end of the day, you're the one playing the game, you have to take the decisions and own them. I've asked caddies what they think about shots, they've told me and then it hasn't been the right decision.

I'm always like, 'Mate, don't worry about it. If you make 20 good calls and one bad one, it's all okay. We're working as a team.'

Of course, there was one difference. Caddies usually get a tournament fee and a tip. I think Jodie just got a really good dinner on the Sunday night!

She's my manager now and that works really well too. Out of everyone I've ever worked with, she's the one who's really got my back and we work together so well. We're going to make some mistakes along the way, I'm sure, but her only interest is in me and us, and she's really good at knowing what I need, even if I don't. If I'm playing a lot of golf, or practising hard as I have been throughout 2023, she knows when I need to rest. She's not afraid to get on the phone and cancel something if she knows it's too much for me.

It's crazy how well we work together. I was in a relationship for nearly ten years before I met her. I came out of that breakup and thought, 'Okay then, it's just me now. Time to focus only on the golf.' And then I've gone out on a weekend, met Jodie and I'm like, 'Oh shit, I'm in love!'

We just clicked. She came out to a tournament in Prague with me, I missed the cut and we had the whole weekend together. We just walked around the city, finding interesting places to eat, drinking and getting to know each other. It was just like we both knew it was going to last. From that moment to now, we've barely spent any time apart. We're always doing everything together, going up to the golf club for a few drinks, going out for dinner. We've even got that column we write together about barbecued meat!

I think every relationship is different. Lots of people do it differently to us, they spend loads of times just with their mates and they keep their lives separate. We just do everything together. We say to people, 'Bring whoever you like, we're not fussed.' This is how we're living our life. And it will stay like this as our daughter grows up.

This isn't to judge other people, I have no interest in doing that. Live and let live. But I don't want to be stuck in a situation where my wife and kid are at home and I'm away for 25 to 35 weeks of the year. Jodie and I are on the same page, we're a team. She's not just my wife, she's my best friend. So is Harley. I can't spend that long apart from them. There's a price to be paid for that, of course, it's three flights all the time and stuff like that. But it's a price worth paying as far as I'm concerned.

I don't want golf to consume me at the expense of having a family. I know of players who have missed the birth of their kids to be at a tournament and while I'm not criticising them, I couldn't do it. I'd feel like I'd lost my perspective if I did that. And as I've proved in the past, it's all too easy to do that.

I want to work hard, I want to play well, I want to win tournaments. But there's a life to live and a world to explore. Jodie loves travelling, while Harley's never been fazed by anything, she loves it. We're just going to embrace it.

Jodie's always the one to give me a slap if I get into bad habits with my golf. She's honest and strong, she's got her feet on the ground and she can always calm me down. I hate to admit it, but she's definitely the smart one in this relationship.

And for someone who never had any interest in the sport, she's really into her golf now. I really liked the fact that she knew nothing about it or me at the start. It was nice. I knew that she liked me for me, and not because I was winning money in big tournaments. But she loves walking a golf course now. People always say to her, 'Do you not get bored just wandering around?' But she's, like, no way, she absolutely loves it.

She's hit a few balls too, she's had a couple of trips to the driving range. But Harley is the one to watch. She's coming up to her fourth birthday as I write this and I always say to her, 'Do you want to come out and hit some golf balls with your daddy?' And every time she'll say yes, she'll swing at one ball with her little club, missing it completely, chuck it on the ground and then go and start digging holes in the sand bunker. And then the other day, something just clicked and she smashed 20 balls, one after the other. She must have just hit that age where the concentration span kicks in, which is great. She's not quite ready to go down to the pitch and putt course like I was, but there's something going on in there.

If she wants to play golf, though, it'll be her decision. We're not going to be pushy parents about it. I'll always ask if she wants to come to the driving range, I'll never tell her that she has to come. I saw too many kids at junior level who might have had a chance if their parents had just laid off them for a bit. None of them stayed in the sport. If she wants to play, I'll be there for her. If she doesn't want to play, no-one's going to force her. Even if I did just buy her a set of miniature clubs …

We didn't expect to have a kid so soon, we hadn't been together a year when we found out Jodie was pregnant, so it was a proper, 'Oh shit!' moment. But it was weird; we were both so chilled and at peace with it so quickly. We didn't worry, we didn't panic. It must have seemed bonkers to everyone else, far too early in the relationship and all that, but to us it was just really amazing and cool.

I started reading all these books about pregnancy and nutrition, trying to make sure that we were doing everything right. The most fascinating thing was watching Jodie as she changed. She's really small and slim, and I just watched her get bigger and bigger. I told her it was probably the only time she was ever going to be fatter than me and amazingly she didn't punch me.

I've never admired anyone more. The way she carried our child just blew my mind. It really did. And all the time it was becoming more real. Especially when it was time to put the furniture together.

There's no pressure like being shit at DIY and having to build a cot. I mean, there is no margin for error there. That's real pressure. That and driving the two of them back from the hospital. I've never been so aware of my driving in my life, it was like doing my test again. Every speed bump we hit, I was like, 'Sorry! Sorry! I'm *so* sorry!' That was the scariest drive ever.

But for the rest of the pregnancy there was no fear at all. It didn't feel rushed, it didn't feel like it was too soon. It just felt natural and right. And I love being a father.

Harley doesn't give a shit if I hit a ball down the fairway and fade it just right. She doesn't give a shit if I miss the cut. What she gives a shit about is whether or not I'm in the front room being Maui out of *Moana*. Then she's happy. She wants me to sing, she wants me to dance, she's not bothered about the golf bit.

But then you've got the mind-fuck bit where you have to remember what's important and yet still remember that you've got to provide for your family. It's a weird split, but you can use it to your advantage. You can compart-mentalise it all and think, right, I'm on the golf course, I need to do this, I need to bring my best. And then when you get home, you need to leave it all behind.

Jodie knows how to put it better. She says, 'When you walk through that door, how do you want Harley to see you? She sees you every day, how do you want to act? How do you want to behave? Do you want to come in in a bad mood because you've had a bad day and be pissed off and in a grump because of a bogey on the 17th? Or do you want to not be that person to your child? Do you want to show her how you cope with disappointment, you shrug it off and you go again?' As usual, she's absolutely right.

Right now, Harley doesn't really understand what I do for a living. I think she knows something is a bit weird, though. She gets really offended when people come up and ask for a picture. She's like, 'Why can't I be in the picture?!'

It's going to be interesting when I'm playing again. She was born into a Covid world and then I've been out for two years, so this will be the first she'll really know of the golf circuit. She's been to a tournament before, though, when she was about 18 months old.

She was sat happily in a golf buggy with some food and she shouted, 'HELLO DADDY!' every time she saw me. But I'm not sure she'll remember that. For now, she's pretty convinced that I'm a professional singer and dancer from *Moana*, and I'm happy to stick with that.

I think I'm a different man now to the way I was before I met Jodie. I think I've got a better grasp of perspective now and I hope that when Harley looks at me, she'll see a better man.

Jon Rahm put it really nicely. He said that he wanted his kids to grow up and not look at what he'd done, but the way that he'd conducted himself. And I think that's so true. That really makes sense. I don't want Harley to look at me and be disappointed in how I've acted.

I want to be there to guide her, but she's going to be a handful. She's already pretty bright, smart enough to outsmart me a few times. But I want to be there to pick her up when she falls, to tell her to have another go. It doesn't matter if you get something wrong, it just matters that you keep going, that you keep trying. And I love the look on her face when I say well done to her. Every parent knows that look. It makes me melt.

I take as much as I can from my memories of my dad and how he encouraged me. And that was the word. It was always encouragement, it was never pushing. And he was always able to provide for us. When I speak to my mum about it, she'll tell me how when times were tough, he'd always come through for us. At one point, he had three jobs at the same time, all for us.

So when I'm sitting there injured, moping around and feeling sorry for myself, I have to give my head a wobble. My dad had three jobs! So I remember that and I get on with it. I crack on. I keep plugging away and I know that I'll get there in the end.

When I look at my childhood, I was so lucky. Dad helped me to try everything. I played tennis, cricket, football, table tennis; whatever I wanted to try, he'd find a way to make it happen. That's how I want to be, I want to be there to support my child. If she feels like she wants to quit, I'll be there to tell her just to take a break, take a few weeks out and come back when you're ready, if you're ready. I don't think it's cool to force stuff on kids. But when she comes back and she has a bad day, I'll be there to pick her up and take her to her favourite restaurant. That's the kind of dad I want to be.

It's weird because they never met each other, but sometimes Jodie says the exact same things to me that my dad said when he was alive. She'll say, 'Come on, you're built to do this. You've got talent.' Or she'll ask me why I would ever consider giving up now when I'm making so much progress.

She's so much like my dad. She'll say, 'I don't care if you never pick up another golf ball again, I'm not going to love you any less. It doesn't matter. But you're stupid if you give up because of *this*.'

I'm a lucky man. Not because I can hit a golf ball, but because I've come from one amazing family into another amazing family. And it all came out of me missing the cut at Wentworth and going out with my caddie to meet some random girls. Mad. Best cut to miss ever!

14

KNOWING BEEF
BY JODIE VALENCIA

I had absolutely no idea who Beef was when I met him. I didn't follow golf at all, but I lived in a house share in Clapham with a girl who was so into it that she'd actually got a selfie with him at Wentworth in 2018. She showed me the picture, but I'd never seen him before in my life. His whole rise to fame in 2016 must have just passed me by completely.

She then matched with his caddie on Tinder and while they were chatting he asked if she wanted to come out and bring her friends along too. Beef, it turned out, had missed the cut and in his own words he wanted to 'go out and get fucked up'.

He was drunk when I first met him. Not catastrophically drunk, but that merry sort of day-drinking drunk where he was just having a really lovely time. I didn't really care that he was a golfer, I wasn't bothered about that at all. I've worked with famous people in the past and it's never really had much of an effect on me. They're just human beings.

But Beef was really good fun and I loved how passionate he was about food and family. They're two of the most important things in my life. So yeah, I liked him from the start.

It was a real sliding doors moment. After all, he didn't miss the cut by much. He did well on the Thursday, but he had a bad day on the Friday. If he'd played well, if he'd turned a couple of bogies into pars, we'd never have met and we'd never have had our daughter Harley together. So maybe it was meant to be?

Looking back, it's easy to say that we were both in the right place, that we were both ready for the next step of our lives, but at the time I was very cautious. I knew that he'd just got out of a long relationship and so we were more like friends than anything else at first. I called him my mate and I wanted to keep him at arm's length. It was a friendship, but then it turned into love. Very soon, I started thinking that I'd met the one, that this was my future husband and I'd never felt like that before about anyone.

The turning point came when he invited me to Prague for the weekend. I had tickets for a festival and I didn't want to let my friends down, but I changed my mind at the last minute, flew out there with him and then fell completely in love with him.

I wasn't worried by the fact that he was a golfer. In fact, it was quite refreshing. I worked in the city, I only ever met people with similar jobs, everyone worked Monday to Friday, nine to five. Beef and I just made it work. It's hard to explain now, but I never really considered the logistics of the whole thing. We were head over heels in love, everything just happened very naturally.

In the beginning, I remember saying that I wasn't ever going to be like his ex-girlfriend and give up my job to travel around the world with him. I'd just been promoted, I was doing really well at work, that would have been mad. But then it became harder and harder to say goodbye to him every time he left for another tournament.

I see life as an adventure, I always have done, and even though we hadn't been together long, everything about us just felt so right.

And so I did it; I actually quit my job and off we went around the world. I just thought, come on then, let's see where this takes us, let's see where this path leads.

I knew I'd be okay. If it didn't work out, I could just get another job and I'd be absolutely fine. But I never thought it would go wrong. I was in love, I was done, I knew that I wanted to be with him. I didn't think about my future, I just thought, well, this is my future NOW.

I remember the first tournament I went to with him. It was the British Masters. We stayed in this lovely hotel and then drove to the golf course every morning. On the first day, I walked all 18 holes with him, we came back to the hotel and as soon as I sat down I fell asleep! I couldn't believe how tired I was. My back was hurting, my calves *were hurting, I was absolutely done in. But it didn't put me off.*

From that moment, I was fully invested in him and the golfing world. I didn't have to do that. I could have just waved him off at the 1st hole and then gone to sit by the pool with a beer, but that didn't seem right. I wanted to be there for him. I wanted to help. I didn't quit my job to just lounge by a swimming pool all day.

Gradually, without even realising it, I basically became his manager. We lived in each other's pockets. From when we became serious at the end of August 2018 to the start of the Covid pandemic, I think we only spent about ten days apart. That must seem really weird to some people. It would have seemed weird to me if you'd told me about that before I met Beef. I know lots of couples where that would be their worst nightmare, couples who really like to give each other their own space, but we're just not like that.

I was there with him through everything. I watched everything, I saw everything. I started to know him better than he knew himself. And very soon I became aware that there was a problem. He was happy every day, but he was also depressed every day, if that makes sense. We laughed together all the time, but he cried too.

When I met him, he was off for a few weeks, he was out of golf mode and just being him. We had such a wonderful summer, going out, travelling the world, eating and drinking and having so much fun. But when he was back on the golf course, I could see this anger rising up inside him and it didn't seem normal.

I wasn't stupid. I know that golf is incredibly frustrating. If he has a bad day out there, he might not get paid. Most people play golf for relaxation, but this wasn't that sort of golf. Even so, it didn't seem right. I was stood quietly off to one side watching and I didn't like what I saw.

At first I was worried that it might be me. I'd think, 'Oh no, should I take this personally? Is he acting like this because I'm here?' It was still a new relationship, it was still at that stage where you question everything.

The world of golf was new to me, but I was very lucky. Some of the other wives and girlfriends were extremely kind to me and told me things about the reality of the sport that I could never have known from the outside. But the more people I met and the more I saw, the more I knew that it wasn't me. My intuition was screaming at me that Beef was in trouble and needed help.

In South Africa later that year, he went out and played well. He played really well and then he came back to the hotel and he cried his heart out. I said to him then that this wasn't right and that he shouldn't be feeling like this. I told him to speak to someone. I knew that if he didn't do it then he was just going to combust. But he resisted it for a while.

I said to him, 'Think about how many hours you're putting into this anger. Think about how much time is going into feeling this way.

'Imagine what else you could do.'

He didn't seem to realise how far he'd come or how well he was doing. He wasn't grateful for anything. I haven't ever been famous, I've never had a really high-pressure job like his, so I could never completely understand what he was going through, but even from the outside I knew what he needed. I knew that there was no problem with us because in the midst of all of this, we still laughed every day. The problem was mental.

I started to throw myself into being there for him. I began to read books about the sport, I talked to as many people as I could, I'd be walking around the golf course making little notes as I went. I found that the best golfers had a different mentality. They were the ones who could take the shot and then leave it alone in the past; they wouldn't take it with them for the next one. Beef and I would speak at the end of every round, like a little debrief.

When it got really bad, he started to strip people out of his life. He didn't want to take anyone down with him, so he told his caddie to find himself a more stable golfer. And that's how I ended up carrying his bag in Dubai. It's funny because I only suggested that I could do it as a joke. I didn't know the first thing about the sport, I'd only just started watching it, but he said, 'Do you want to?' and so I did.

They had to get a smaller bag for me and even that was almost as big as me. I didn't know any of the right words to say or how to behave. It was this whole new vocabulary of 'pars' and 'pins' and stuff. But amazingly, we did really well together.

I think I just took him out of his head for a bit. I tried to get him laughing and joking while he was out there. I couldn't tell him the right club to use, but I could just get him to stop taking it all so seriously. I said to him, 'What's the worst that can happen out there? You're playing golf for fuck's sake. You're not swimming with crocodiles. What's riding on this? What does it matter?'

I said to him that if it all went wrong and it all fell away, we'd be okay. We'd still have each other and we'd find something else to do. It wasn't like he was going to die out there on the golf course. And so he had fun instead. He played really well and he told me it was the most fun he'd had out there in ages.

But that was only ever going to be a temporary fix. We went to Australia and unfortunately it all got the better of him. He was in a bunker, he took too many swings trying to get out of it and he hadn't learned how to deal with that short fuse. It was all too much. He was like, 'Fuck it!' And that was it.

But at least that day helped make him see that he had to seek professional help. There was so much going on in there. It wasn't just the golf and the fame. I don't know if he ever really dealt with the death of his dad. The more we spoke, the more I was able to break down the barriers. He's a man, so he was always going to resist, he was always going to try to put up defences and hold it all in. But his dad died and that left a hole in his life. His dad was such a big influence on him, but he never saw his son become a golfer, he never saw his son win a tournament. That's a lot to carry around with you.

I don't think anyone was to blame for what happened to him. It's easy to look at the people around him, but Beef wouldn't even be playing now if it hadn't been for his first manager getting him back out on the golf course. He put his money where his faith in Beef was and he got him moving in the right direction.

But I just don't think there was anyone in his life in 2016 with the experience to deal with such a rapid rise to fame. That sort of thing hardly ever happens, he came out of nowhere. But the fall came as fast as the rise. He was 75th in the world in 2017, but he'd slipped to 175th by the time he met me and, as I write this after he's spent two years out injured, he's currently 1,892nd.

But he's turned it around before and he'll turn it around again. When we discovered that I was pregnant, he was playing brilliantly. Before Harley was born, he'd got himself back into the top 150 and he was really enjoying his golf again. He'd missed out on Dubai in 2018, but after all that time working on himself, he'd done enough to qualify for it in 2019.

The fact that he chose to be with me for Harley's birth instead of playing in those lucrative tournaments tells you all you need to know about his values. I think there's nothing more important than family and I never doubted where he'd be for a moment.

He's never been about the money. He doesn't play golf for that, he plays golf because he loves it.

It's his passion and he's good at it. The money is just a bonus.

He's changed so much in the time I've known him. When I see footage of him from 2016, he's got this startled look, like a deer caught in the headlights. But he's fought and won so many battles now, he's a husband and a father. He's come through these things, he's overcome them and he's built resilience now. He's grown and he's evolved.

On the surface, he's still the same Beef that everyone thinks they know, full of laughs and jokes. But underneath, he's much more mature. He's more understanding, more accepting of himself, he's got more perspective, he cares a bit less about the outcome and a bit more about the process. There's still some fire and aggression in there, of course, and I have no doubt that there will be frustration too, but he's better able to cope with it now.

Neither of us have really had time to take stock of everything that happened. We've had this whirlwind romance, we've travelled the world, we've had a baby, we've been through Covid, we've been through his injury. I always have to tell him to just slow down and reflect on everything that's happened.

I think I understand what happened to him in 2017. He wasn't ready. He went to America, but he didn't go out with the right support. Everyone wanted a piece of him and the pressure got to him. I think it will be different now. Especially with me by his side.

I know him better than any manager. I'm not an agent motivated by getting my 10 per cent. I know what he needs, I can be more objective in judging what he should do and what he should say no to. I know that some people will judge me as some sort of freak who's obsessed with her husband, but I really see us as a team now. I see us being more like Lee Westwood and Helen Storey, a couple working together and leaning on each other. We have a level of trust that's not always easy to find in other people. We've certainly been burned in the past on that front.

I'd like to go back to the caddying too, but there's no hurry, especially with Harley still so young. Anyway I'm still mortified by something that happened out there. I was really conscious that I didn't know the etiquette and I was really nervous about embarrassing him when we were out there. I was trying to look really engaged with it all, not least because it was one of the tournaments where the fans can get really close to you, so we were walking around with this big crowd. I was trying to play the part, staring down the fairway with a serious look on my face, acting like I really knew what I was talking about.

'What are you hitting here?' I asked him, all serious. He looked at me and just creased up laughing.

'What's wrong?' I said.

'You've got chocolate all over your face!'

I'm such a messy eater. I've got a really small mouth and I blame it all on that. I'd eaten this protein bar and ended up just smearing it all over myself. All of the spectators heard him and started laughing too. I just wanted the ground to swallow me up.

But who knows? He played well that day, so maybe I should go round with chocolate all over my face every time.

15

THE GREATEST COURSES

I've been lucky enough to play on some of the greatest golf courses in some of the most incredible locations on earth, but North Middlesex will always be the one closest to my heart. It's cheating, to be fair – it's not really a golf course to me, it's more like a second home.

It's the first place I want to go whenever I'm back in England. I've known people there for over 20 years, they're not members, they're friends, so it's a very special place for me.

I feel a bit bad that when I did a video there with John Robbins, my podcast co-host, we didn't exactly show the course in its best light. We couldn't have picked a worse time to do it. They were aerating the greens at the time, punching little holes in them to keep them healthy, so they all looked like Tommy Lee Jones's face. My mate is the head greenkeeper there, so I can give him some shit if the course isn't perfect, but that wasn't his fault and it usually looks amazing.

It's funny, though; you'd think after the number of times I've played it, I'd be getting amazing scores, but it's the most frustrating golf course ever. It's only 5,500 yards long, so it's tiny and there are lots of par fours where you can drive onto the green with your first shot. But if you hit it even slightly off line, you'll put it in someone's kitchen because the course is surrounded by flats. I've seen too many shots that get given a bit too much and disappear over the trees. It's horrible, everyone goes silent and cringes, waiting for the smash of broken glass. The people who live near the 3rd must have loyalty cards with the local glaziers. They've been absolutely peppered over the years.

The one course that I've always wanted to play is Augusta, that's at the top of my bucket list. Everyone I know who has played in the Masters has told me how amazing it is to play there, how it's even better in real life. It's manicured to absolute perfection.

I was lucky enough to play Leopard Creek recently. It's a brilliant golf course anyway, but it's built on the side of the Kruger National Park so it's filled with wildlife. When you walk onto the 13th, a par five, there's this river by the green. It's called Crocodile River, which is the sort of thing that can stop you from dawdling on your putt. It's mostly hippos there. And I know because on all four days I marked my ball and went for a sneaky look. Sometimes it was elephants, sometimes it was giraffes. You don't get that at North Mid, to be fair.

I'm not usually keen on wildlife on the golf course, though. I'm terrible with that sort of thing. I'm from

London, we're not used to interesting wildlife. The most dangerous things we've got there are wasps. I remember playing at Sun City once and the officials told me to hold back as I was approaching the tee box. They didn't look very happy. It turned out there was a massive black mamba by the tees and they'd had to bring in specialist snake catchers to deal with it. That's the last thing you need if you're feeling nervous about your tee shot.

Lake Karrinyup is another amazing golf course – it's in Perth, Australia and you get kangaroos on the fairways. But I remember playing there on the front nine and there was this par five that ran around the outside of a lake. I was on the fairway, laying up my second shot and I saw this absolutely massive snake slithering across the fairway, 200 yards away. It was huge. I didn't want to take the shot, I was scared I might hit him and make him angry. You had to feel for the ball spotters, though. One lad was sat on a chair in front of a bush, looking out towards the green, when a massive one came sliding out under his chair, straight between his legs. And this was no grass snake, it was one of the poisonous ones. This was not the sort of golf course where you want to be poking around in the undergrowth looking for your ball. In fact, they've got signs up specifically telling you that if you hit your ball into a bush, it's gone. Don't even bother trying to retrieve it, it's not worth it.

There was a story last year about some golfers at the Coast Golf Club in Sydney who found a poisonous red-bellied black snake coiled up in the hole on the 2nd.

He was four foot long, but he'd somehow got himself in there, probably to get away from the sun. The golfers, it was reported, decided to award themselves both a two-putt and move on. I don't blame them. I wouldn't want to mess with that.

I've played on a few courses with alligators too. I was practising in Florida a few years back, down in Sarasota, and I was down at the back of the range by the lake, hitting balls. Suddenly I could hear this weird noise, like a heavy grunting sound. I was with Jodie and I said to her, 'That has got to be an alligator.'

We went to take a look and I was right. It was absolutely enormous, like a fucking dinosaur, lifting itself out of the lake and grunting over and over again. It didn't look real, it's like one of those stop-motion monsters from old movies. You don't want to mess with those guys. It turned out that he was making a mating call, giving it the universal message of, 'My parents are out! Come on over!' We didn't stick around for that bit, though.

It does remind you how lucky you are to do this for a living. Humans have put golf courses all over the planet and so many of them are next to nature reserves or the wilderness. There are courses in Canada and the United States where you occasionally get bears coming out onto the greens. That's an amazing sight.

But with some golf courses, you don't need lots of wildlife to take your breath away. Pebble Beach is one of the most astonishing golf courses I've ever seen. It's all about the layout. It's right on the west coast of California, literally built into the clifftops, and sticks out to sea in some places. The greens are small and fast and severe, so you have to be so smart about where you put your ball. The views are incredible, but that wouldn't mean much if the course was shit. Fortunately, this course is amazing.

The 7th hole is a short par three where you either hit the ball on the green, get lucky and drop it in a bunker or get unlucky and watch in horror as it rolls off the side of a steep cliff into the ocean. And it's hard not to be distracted because you're hitting into the wind as it comes off the ocean and the view is absolutely stunning.

There's another golf course close by called Cypress Point, but it's a very private club and access is extremely limited. It was designed by Alister MacKenzie, the same genius behind Augusta, and it's supposed to be every bit as good. But the only way you can play is if you're one of the 250 members or if you're invited by one of the 250 members. And even if you're invited to join, which is pretty unlikely, you'll have to stump up $250,000 to pay the initial fee. Bob Hope and Ben Hogan used to be members, Clint Eastwood still plays there apparently. I'm not sure I'll be able to get into that one. And I bet they have weird rules about shoes there …

There will always be something special about St Andrews, home of the Royal & Ancient Golf Club. It's right next to the town, for starters, so you could be staying in a hotel there and you've only got a five-minute walk to the tee.

It's such a wild course, as like so many of the old links courses it's basically been designed by nature. No-one's dug up land, no-one's planted special flowers to look pretty for the TV cameras, it just goes out into the wilds and comes back again. Some of the greens are so vast that they're used for more than one hole: you've got the 2nd and 16th hole on the same one, for example. And there's such an incredible aura about the 17th and the 18th, it's hard to explain what it is.

You play on this course that is as barren and wild as Augusta is beautiful and cultivated, and then you approach the end. You cross the Swilcan Bridge, that tiny stone crossing over the burn, and you head back towards those beautiful buildings, the same way thousands of golfers have for nearly two hundred years. It really gets to you.

And it's not easy to play those courses, especially when the weather is a factor. I remember the Dunhill Links at Carnoustie one year. It was October, I was having a bit of breakfast and the rain was coming down, but I figured it might clear as the day brightened up. The day did not brighten up. It was dark, properly dark all morning. The flags were bent over double in the wind, the rain was coming in sideways and I was like, 'Fuck that.'

I just wanted to put the kettle on, have a cup of tea, maybe get the board games out. The last thing I wanted to do was go out and play golf. But the best I could do was to skip the warm-up, have another cup of tea and just go straight out to the first tee without hitting any balls. That was a long day.

You never know what the weather's going to do when you're up in Scotland, so even the most straightforward-looking links course can suddenly turn against you. A lot of people don't like that, but I think it keeps you on your toes. You get some holes where the wind is behind you and you've got to take a bit off, you get vicious crosswinds where you have to select your shots carefully, it's great fun. Even if sometimes you do wish you were back in Florida …

My favourite golf courses are the ones that have real definition. You know, the ones where the greens are green and smooth, where the fairway looks like a fairway and the rough looks rough. It's just really pleasing on the eye as all the colours contrast against each other. And I also hate a long par three.

I think you can get some good ones, some where you're hitting a mid iron in, but there should be a limit. The best par threes are the ones where it's like a shootout, you're dropping it 120 yards or so, straight onto the green. Hopefully.

If you look at the 17th at Sawgrass, that's 130 yards and that's a great hole. The Postage Stamp at Troon is even shorter, it's just 110 yards, and that gorgeous 7th at Pebble Beach is only just over 100 yards.

I don't like to give the man credit, but Donald Trump's course in Dubai has got four brilliant par threes, all about 150 yards with fiddly little greens and dangerous slopes. They're brilliant because they're so risky. You can put any pro on the tee for one of them, put a nine iron in their hand and watch them struggle to compose themselves. It's a mental battle because you know what can go wrong. Sure, you can get a hole in one on these, but you can also give it just a little bit too much and drop right off the end of the green. That nine iron can feel like a six iron sometimes, loaded up with too much power.

And even if you get the length right, if you get the line even slightly wrong, you can end up in a bunker, trying to chip it out somewhere near the hole to rescue a par. It's exciting for us, and it's exciting for the spectators as well.

I love a par five too, especially when it's designed to offer a balance of risk and reward. One of those ones that you know you can take it on if you land your tee shot on the fairway. I love it when you have to make that call. I want that moment of indecision where you have to get your head together. 'Fuck, I'm 180 yards away.'

If I take out an iron and put it on the green with my second shot, I've got a chance at an eagle and I really should get a birdie at the very least. 'Come on, you've got to be hitting a six iron into this green.' And then you take the shot and you miss the green and you're right in the shit and you're beating yourself up.

Going for the green is a big risk: you might miss it and end up in deep rough or behind a tree or something. But if you give up on the eagle, opt to get it down the fairway and then wedge it onto the green from closer range, as you'll have a much higher chance of a birdie. But then there's no chance of an eagle. Fuck! All the best golf courses have those holes that get your brain whirring and force you to balance out common sense with properly reckless courage.

Some courses have great big wide fairways for their par fives, so you know you're going to land on them because it's so difficult to hit the rough. Then you look up and see a vast expanse of green and so you get a three wood out and blast it on without worrying too much. That's just too safe.

I definitely don't want any gimmicks. I only recently discovered what a condor was and it just sounds crazy. A hole in one on a par five, one step up from the lesser spotted albatross, which is a hole in one on a par four, or getting through a par five in two. Apparently only five people have ever got a condor and only two of them sound genuine. One was in Devon and was the result of going over a hedge on a horseshoe-shaped hole and then getting a very favourable bounce. The other was in Denver at a golf course a mile above sea level where the air is thin and the balls travel much further. But even with that altitude, he still hit it over 500 yards, so it must have had some serious wind behind it too. It's all a bit daft.

To be honest I'm more concerned with getting a hole in one on a par four. With some of the holes at North Mid, I should have managed one by now, but as I always say with stuff like this, it's hard enough getting the ball down from ten foot, let alone 400 yards. Anyway, that's not the stuff that makes a golf course great; it's designing something that leaves the golfer worrying about every decision, always wondering if they should go for it or play it safe.

That's the stuff that the course designers need to worry about. Not what the view is like or what colour the flowers are or where the water feature should go. The greatest golf courses should keep you second guessing yourself all the time.

Funnily enough I was invited to this golf show once and I was asked to design my perfect hole. So I got up there and obviously I wanted a 140-yard par three. So I drew the little tee box at the bottom and then I had the fairway stretching out curving off to the right and then a big round green. And that's when I realised that I'd basically drawn a massive upside-down cock on the paper. That's when it crossed my mind that perhaps golf course design might not be for me.

But one golf course that I'll always love is Valderrama in Andalucía, in Spain. It's the course that hosted the 1997 Ryder Cup, the Andalucía Masters on the DP World Tour (as the European Tour is now called), and the course where I won my first event.

It gets mixed reviews from some golfers. There's a lot of people out there who hate it because it's a hard golf course, but I love it. It's a real shame that it's not on the tour now because it's such a lovely course to play. It's got that definition that I love, it's always in such perfect condition. It's not too long, so you don't end up walking miles; it's just over 6,500 yards, which is just about right.

The reason I think I play well there, and please don't laugh as I'm absolutely serious, is that Valderrama is actually a lot like North Mid. It's not long, you've got to think carefully about what you're doing, there's lots of strategy and it will punish you if you take it lightly.

I've been there before when people have got drivers out on certain holes and I'm there with my three iron thinking, 'Yeah, I'm going careful on this one and I'll see how you do because if you get that driver even slightly off line, you're going in the undergrowth and I'll be happily wedging onto the green'. Such a great strategic golf course and, yeah, I'll always love going back there.

16

MY GOLFING HEROES

Not a lot of people realise, but I'm actually mixed race. My dad was half Jamaican. On his side of the family, most of my cousins have much darker skin, but for some reason me, my brother and my sister have both got very light skin. It used to be really funny, I'd meet up with my cousins and play football and people would say, 'Who the fuck is that white kid?' and they'd be told that I was family and they wouldn't believe it.

But that's not why Tiger Woods is my favourite player of all time. And it's not because he's a working-class kid who broke down boundaries in a sport that had always been closed off to people like him. I didn't really appreciate those things until I was older.

No, the reason I loved watching Tiger Woods play was because he was so fucking good at golf. He just changed the game completely. Some of the shots he hit, the power he got on the ball, the way he worked the crowd. Growing up in that era, seeing him at his peak as he dominated the sport so profoundly, it was just pure excitement.

I used to watch tournaments with my dad and we'd be saying, 'Who's going to even get close to him this time?' In my head, it was always Tiger versus the rest of the field.

I'll never forget meeting him, but even just seeing him at tournaments used to blow my mind. He'd be walking around with 40 or 50 people surrounding him at any given time, everyone wants a piece of him. Even in the locker room, which is supposed to be your safe space, your refuge from all the madness, even in there, you'd get other players coming up and asking him for a selfie. I used to feel quite sorry for him, really, it seemed like a very difficult way to live your life. I never asked him for anything, I just let him be.

But then I bumped into him in 2018 at the US Open. I'd got there early, I went out to the range first thing to get some practice in and he was just coming off, which tells you everything you need to know about his work ethic.

I didn't really know what to say, so I went with a casual nod and a simple, 'What's up, Tiger!' And he looked at me and he said, 'What up, big boy?'

Imagine that. The first thing the greatest golfer of all time ever says to you is, 'What up, big boy?' Magnificent. How cool is that?

We had a little chat, I told him how great it was to see him back on the golf course because he'd suffered from a few injuries (though they paled in comparison with what he would suffer in 2021 when he nearly lost a leg in a car crash) and he wished me all the best, told me to keep doing what I was doing. Oh, and he congratulated me on a sponsorship deal I'd just agreed with the burger chain Arby's, so that was pretty awesome too!

It was so bizarre to have someone you've grown up watching just stop and talk to you about the golf. I'll never get used to stuff like that. But I think everyone is like that with him to some extent. I've heard Rory McIlroy talk about him and how well he hits his irons. I mean, have you seen Rory play? He's a ridiculous golfer, there's hardly anyone who hits his irons like Rory. And even he is talking about Tiger like he's on another level. Sometimes I can lose ages on YouTube just watching compilations of his best shots, and I doubt I'm the only professional golfer who's done that. He does things that no-one else can do.

I'm not usually one for statistics, but there's two that really stick out for me. So, you know how all the way through this book I've told you how hard golf is and how fine the line is between success and failure? I've told you about the times I've missed the cut. If you go back through old leaderboards, you'll see that missing the cut isn't unusual. It's not what you want, but even if you're one of the best players in the world, you'll still miss the cut from time to time.

Unless you're Tiger Woods between 1998 and 2005, that is. In those seven years, he made the cut *142 times consecutively*. That is fucking mind-blowing.

Here's another for you. From 1997 to 2013, Woods was a combined 126 under par in Major championships. The next on the list is Steve Flesch and he's 125 *over*. Phil Mickelson, one of the greatest players of the last 30 years, is 128 over. And Tiger is out there 251 strokes in front on his own. And this is the Majors, the time when the pressure is most intense. No-one does that. No-one should be capable of doing that. It's barely human. When you speak to his old coaches, they'll tell you that he was so good at one point that he was winning tournaments even when he was off his game. I genuinely don't think we'll ever see a golfer of his calibre ever again.

I think every player would tell you that if they could be paired with anyone at a tournament, they'd want it to be Tiger. I've never had it yet. He was injured a lot when I was playing the Majors and doing really well, so I never had the opportunity to play with him. In fairness, it probably wouldn't have done my golf any good, but it would have been an amazing experience.

I wish I'd gone over and spoken to him more, I wish I'd asked him a bit about how he played, but I always felt a bit like it wasn't right. That he was in the locker room, doing his thing and he should be left alone. But hopefully he'll get back out there soon and our paths will cross.

It's astonishing that he's even able to consider playing a round of golf. After the car crash it was touch and go as to whether he'd even get to keep his leg. He's had spinal surgery. And he still came back afterwards to make the cut at the Masters and finish in the top 30. I know that he's won all those Majors and all those tournaments, but to come back after that accident and to even be able to compete at that level has to be one of the greatest achievements of his career. He shouldn't be playing golf, it shouldn't be possible, and I don't even know how he's walking. But that's the man. You can never write him off. I think every golfer who is playing now owes him a debt of gratitude for what he's done for the sport.

But before Tiger came along, I think my first hero of golf was Chi-Chi Rodríguez, a guy from Puerto Rico who was at his best in the 1960s and 1970s. He was amazing, he had this celebration where he brandished his golf club like a sword and did a Zorro dance before sliding it back into an imaginary sheath. That's awesome.

He was a groundbreaking player, he came from nowhere. He started caddying because he made more money from that than his old job, he practised with tin cans and when he got a chance to swing a real club, he turned out to be amazing at it.

I think I was always drawn to the entertainers, the people who played with a smile on their face as if they'd realised it was the greatest way to make a living and it wasn't actually an awful chore. I love that sort of showman.

Miguel Ángel Jiménez used to do the sword dance as well. I've never had the bottle to do it myself for real, I think I'm more at home with a flying chest bump, but I played with Jiménez at the Scottish Open and holed out for an eagle on the 18th. It was a wedge shot from about 80 yards and it went straight in the hole, a lovely way to finish the third day. I couldn't resist it, I was flicking the club around and dancing, and he loved it. He came over and gave me a big hug and celebrated with me. The funniest thing, though, was that the clip ended up on *A Question of Sport* a few months later, so I was getting sent it by my mates. I was featured on *Question of Sport* for my dancing before I was invited on for my golf. Oh, and by the way, I got my home question correct. That was a nerve-wracking moment. You can't get that one wrong.

And then there was John Daly. I've spoken a bit about his fashion style, but it was his total style that I loved. He was unbelievably talented, but lived by his own rules. And boy, could he hit a golf ball. Imagine what he could do if he was at his physical peak now with the equipment we use these days. He'd be smacking it into a different time zone.

To generate that much power every time was phenomenal, but he was so much more than a big driver. His short game was brilliant too. I played with him a few times and his shots around the green were amazing.

I saw him on the putting green when we were playing in Germany and we had a little chat. He was really polite, we spoke about the tournament and then I left him to his preparation. But a couple of years later I saw him in Turkey and I figured that I had to go up and speak to him properly.

'Are we gonna have a beer or what?' I said to him. And he was like, 'Yeah, sure, I'll have a beer.' And so he got this massive bucket of beers and we drank them all and started to put the world to rights. But we weren't finished.

So he said, 'Come back to my hotel, we'll have another drink,' and he wasn't joking. We got back there and he ordered two large whiskys and Coke, but when they brought them over they were basically highball glasses full of whisky and ice with room for about 30 ml of Coke if you had a steady hand. And I thought to myself, 'Fuck, I am in trouble here.'

It was an amazing night, we talked loads, he's such a good bloke with a such a big heart, but unfortunately I can't really remember much of it apart from the bit later on when I realised I'd taken off all of my clothes and was shouting about jumping in the swimming pool.

We still see each other now and have a laugh about it. Whenever I'm in the USA, I drop him a line to see if he's around and if he wants to play some golf. I take people as I find them and he's always been incredible to me. He's one of those people that, if you need something, he'd always be there. Whether you were Tiger Woods or just me, he'd show up. He's a very cool man.

He's always had a reputation for heavy drinking and that's not something I ever went into with him. I don't like to ask famous people the same sort of questions that journalists would want to ask, if you know what I mean. I've always been a bit wary about that. I'd rather just chat about the golf.

But I have a lot of sympathy for his situation. We played in Florida a few years back and went out for dinner afterwards. We'd gone to this place and there were people who were coming up to him, not for autographs or selfies, but to try to do a shot with him. Sometimes they wouldn't leave any margin for error, they'd just buy a load of shots and come over, or challenge him to a chug-a-beer contest. They weren't doing it because they were bad people or anything, they were just looking for a good time and I get that. But the peer pressure was intense. You could see the sort of cycle he could find himself on.

But all of that 'Wild Thing' stuff only detracts from what a great player he was. And he was great. He came out of nowhere, he won two Majors, he tore courses up and drove harder and further than anyone else at the time. He was a course designer's worst nightmare. And even now, he's still out there on senior tours and still hitting it over 300 yards. What a guy.

There are a couple of guys whose peak came a little bit before my time, but who made an impact on me anyway. I've seen footage of Seve Ballesteros and he was amazing. To come out of Spain and dominate the USA in the way that he did was incredible. But to do it all with a smile on his face was something else. Not that you should let that fool you, though. I've spoken to people in the game who describe Seve as one of the toughest competitors who has ever played the game. He used to say, 'You walk on that tee, you shake their hand, you smile and then you have to be ready to beat them. You have to be ready to destroy them.' And that's the way he played.

When I had that run-in with that radio station, it was one of the most miserable days of my time in the sport. But I was really moved when Sir Nick Faldo stepped in to support me. That was an incredible moment because he's one of the finest golfers that this country has ever produced. He had an extraordinary mentality and an ice-cold composure even in the toughest moments.

He also rebuilt his entire swing midway through his career, which is crazy. That's such a huge risk to take. Those muscle patterns are so heavily ingrained, it's really tough to override them, chuck them all out and start again. People thought he was crazy because usually you hit a level in golf and then you just have areas that you can refine and improve, little subtle changes, because there's not really an off season where you can do serious work on your game.

But he wanted to change everything. He wasn't happy with the way that he'd played or the way he'd fallen short in a few tournaments. He wanted to be able to hit every fairway, to hit every green, to not make mistakes where it would cost him. And he decided that this was the only way he could do it.

And he did it. He just went out and did it the only way you can; by hitting hundreds and hundreds of golf balls day after day after day. That mentality was incredible and that's why he won so many Majors.

I think every golfer would love to have that mentality. That grittiness, that unflappable nature. I'm sure that some things did bother him, but it never looked like that was the case. He'd spar with journalists in press conferences, he'd put up with negative headlines, but nothing ever stopped him from achieving his ambitions. He was in his own little bubble and he was the king of it.

I've spoken to him a few times and he's such a strong character. I'm not surprised that he was such a popular pundit in the USA because he's not someone who minces his words. And when you've achieved as much as he has, you don't have to. He's strong minded, you don't get any bullshit with him and I'm really glad to have such a good relationship with him. I certainly wouldn't want to be his enemy!

One of the most interesting people in golf is Padraig Harrington; he's a genius in his own right. I've already mentioned the way that he experimented with the Happy Gilmore drive, but it's not just that. He thinks deeply about every aspect of the game, he's constantly striving for a new advantage, some way of snatching a marginal gain.

I don't know why I didn't do it earlier in my career, but recently I've started trying to make the most of my opportunity to pick the finest brains in golf. I saw Padraig in 2023 and had a chat with him, and I'm usually a bit shy about stuff like this, but I plucked up the courage to say, 'We've played together a few times. Where do I need to improve? What can I do to get better?'

He looked at me for a second and I could tell that he was weighing up whether to just say something nice or to be honest with me.

And he went with honesty.

'Beef,' he said. 'You hit the ball great, you're just as good as anyone at that bit. But you need to massively improve your short game, that's the bit that needs to be a whole lot better. It's not just about spending time practising bunker shots every morning, or anything like that. That gets really boring really quickly. What you need to do is just play games and develop ideas and try things. If you work on that short game and you get better there, your scores will improve and you'll start heading up the leaderboard.'

He was the first leading golfer that I'd had that conversation with and I just wish I'd had it earlier. It was good, honest and open feedback and it's the sort of thing I needed, especially from someone like him.

One golfer I'd love to chat to about this is Brett Rumford, the Australian. I once watched him practise from the bunker and it was like watching a circus act in training. He was dropping the ball in the same place again and again and again, but with three different shots on rotation. First, he's hit one that's gone up out of the sand, bounced and spun back a foot or two to the hole. Then he's hit one that's just plopped down near the hole, then he's pitched one short that's bounced and rolled forward to the hole. I was watching the man do this for 20 minutes and it was extraordinary. He's based in Perth, and I was so tempted to go out and see him when I was in Singapore.

Luke Donald's putting game is amazing. I spoke to him about it and his advice was to work really hard on 12-foot putts and then anything outside of that was just speed and control. So I used to hit loads and loads of long putts across greens, across slopes, always working on that speed and control. He said, 'If your speed and control are good, you're never going to be too far away. And if you just get it close, you're going to get it on the next one.'

It's simple stuff, but he said that's what he did. Again and again and again, just work your 12-footers, take the pressure off, leave yourself lots of short ones. It works.

When I was younger, I didn't take the opportunity to ask these questions. I was just like, 'I'm here, let's go!' I wanted to get my head down and play my golf. But as you get older, you start to look around, and you see the amazing players you're out there alongside and you just want to pick up as much as you can. And as I write this at the end of 2023 with my DP World Tour comeback looming up ahead of me, I'm out there practising every day, putting all this to good use.

One of the players I admire the most is someone who is much less well known. Matteo Manassero was the wonder kid of golf back in 2010. He won four European Tour events before his 20th birthday, he was an absolutely phenomenal player. And then it all went wrong. He really started to struggle with the mental side of the game and he went to pieces. He lost his tour card, dropped down the ladder and at one point it looked as if he might never play again, which is wild for someone who was so successful at such a young age.

He spent five years off the tour, but he managed to turn it all around and get himself back up for the 2024 season after a successful year on the Challenge Tour. It's a phenomenal story and it really tells you how tough this sport can be to people. I've known him for years, I played with him when I was 17 and he was 13. He'd be absolutely smashing it, hitting his three wood more accurately than I could hit a seven iron onto the green, and all you could do was look at him and think, 'Fuck! He's going to be good!'

It was great to catch up with him recently and congratulate him on his return to the tour. He's a lovely guy, he's been on his own journey and I'm just so pleased that he's back.

I've known Rory McIlroy for years too, as we grew up playing at the same level in the boys' tournaments. I got paired with him at an amateur tournament at the Forest of Arden once and just really got on with him. I think his dad was caddying for him and my sister was caddying for me. Some people allow success to change them, but I have so much respect for Rory because that's never happened to him. He's an absolute superstar, but it doesn't matter. He's the same Rory.

I saw him in Dubai recently and it's the same every time. We have a bit of a chat, ask about each other's families and have a laugh.

He's just a real top man. He's got very strong values, a very clear idea of how things should be and he's not afraid to share his thoughts, as a lot of people in golf have realised.

It hasn't been easy for him recently. He came out really strong against LIV Golf and in favour of the PGA and then got completely blindsided when they announced a merger. I wanted to message him and just say, 'Forget it, mate. Concentrate on your own goals, go and win all the tournaments you can possibly win. Don't even get involved with that shit, it just drains you.'

But you can't stop him. He's passionate about golf, he's passionate about the way he feels golf should conduct itself and what it should represent. He's just trying to protect those ideals. But I hope it doesn't distract people from how good a golfer he is, because he is some player. One of the best in the world without a doubt.

But nobody will ever come close to Tiger Woods. I honestly think he's the best there will ever be. Better than Jack Nicklaus, better than Ben Hogan, better than Arnold Palmer. There will never be anyone as brilliant as Tiger.

17

PUTTING

Putting is, by some distance, the most potentially difficult part of a day at the golf course. You can tee off brilliantly, you can have great approach play, but if you screw up your putting game, it can break you.

It's the most frustrating part of the sport by far when you play six or seven perfect holes and you hit every fairway and you get a few good shots in on the green and you still haven't made a decent putt. It's a real test of your mental strength. But on the days when it goes well, on the days when you just feel like you cannot miss … those are the best days on a golf course.

There's something I've always found quite interesting about putting. People will be a bit weirded out by this, but stick with me. I can tell a really, really good putter by the way the ball goes in the hole. Seriously. They hit the ball in a certain way where the roll is so good on the ball that when it goes in the hole, I find that it dips into the hole quicker, almost like it's meant to be there.

It's like an optical illusion and when I try to explain this to people, they're all like, 'What the fuck are you on about, Beef?'

But then I speak to coaches and they say they know what I mean.

It's the way they hit it. When it goes over the edge of the hole it just seems to dip a bit faster. I've seen it with Luke Donald, I've seen it with John Daly. One hundred per cent, I'm telling you that it's a thing. I've even done it myself when I've been playing really, really well, where I can feel it and I can visually see it going into the hole in a different way. It's like when you're playing football and you catch a volley just right off the top of your laces and you know it's going into the top corner.

In fact, it's a bit like those free-kicks that Ronaldo used to take for Manchester United. He'd step up and strike it so perfectly that the ball would go up and down and wobble and then before the goalkeeper knows what's happened, it's behind him. Except in this case, the ball is struck so perfectly, so square and so flush, that it just zips away and into the hole, like it was born to do it. That's what you're trying to achieve, that's the holy grail.

You can hear it too. It's a different pitch, a different click off the face of the putter. And it's the best feeling in the world. Honestly, you just stand there, you hit the putt, it goes exactly where you aimed it and it's the greatest feeling in the world.

Unfortunately, it's also the easiest thing in the world to fuck up.

But this is one of the great things about the sport. Golf is hard, but it's hard for everyone. If you've ever had one of those days on the green where you've landed on the green, five feet from the hole and then needed four putts to get it down … well, I have good news. Get yourself on YouTube, there are compilation videos of millionaire professional golfers doing exactly the same. I'll watch them every now and then, it's probably bad karma to have a laugh, but you can't help it, it's funny. And it happens to everyone.

You're hitting a small ball with a small bit of metal on a stick into a small hole across an uneven surface made up of thousands of tiny green spikes. There's a lot that can go wrong.

It can be really, really fine margins too. Like, you only have to hit it a little too hard to mess it up. Or a little too soft. Or a little too off.

And even when you get it right, you might get it wrong. I've seen tests where they've rolled the ball across the green the same way again and again and it's only gone down seven times out of ten. It's never quite the same every time. But you will be your own biggest enemy out there.

If you don't take your time, if you don't consider the possibilities, if you don't aim it properly, if you just walk up and hit it and your club face is slightly open or slightly closed, it will go wrong. There's very little margin for error.

When you think about it, it's a really difficult thing to do. Where are you right now while you're reading this?

The living room? The bedroom? If someone put a coffee mug on its side at the other end of the room and asked you to roll a golf ball into it with your hand, could you do it first time? If you're reading this in the loo, then yes, you probably could. But in any other room, I'm not sure you'd do it first time. And we're talking about a similar sort of challenge, but outside from further away and you can't use your hand, you have to use a stick. It's mad, really.

And it's hard enough on your local golf course. But when you're playing for your living, it's even worse. I had one in Houston, Texas, where I didn't play too well, but I was scrambling around and just needed an uneventful final hole to make the cut for the weekend. I three-putted it and missed the cut by one. That one really hurt because, as I said earlier on, if you miss the cut, you don't get paid. You've just spent two days and thousands of pounds on travel and hotels and it was all for nothing because you couldn't put a fucking ball down a fucking hole from three feet away.

Those are the things that you just have to shut out of your head straightaway. You have to move on. You can be brilliant one day and terrible the next. And it can happen to anyone.

I saw it happen to this kid at the Phoenix Open once. It wasn't the worst putting I've ever seen, but it was definitely the worst place to do it. If you know the TPC Scottsdale, you'll know the 16th hole, the stadium hole. It's like a Roman colosseum, it's the closest that golf will ever get to a football match. It's 25,000 Americans who literally run to their seats at 7 a.m. and start drinking. Everyone is smashed and rowdy as fuck. And it's Friday afternoon when me and this guy I'm playing with, a qualifier at his first PGA event, rock up.

I'm all right. I've chipped the ball up and putted it for a par. He had a 30-foot shot down the hill and he left it about four feet short. I'm all done, so I'm standing there watching. And it all goes quiet, almost as if the crowd sort of know on some level what's going to happen. And he misses it, goes four feet past and the crowd goes wild. And then it all goes quiet. And he misses it, goes four feet past and the crowd goes wild. And I nudge my caddie and I was like, 'This is brutal, imagine if he misses again.' And he missed again and honestly, the eruption from those fans, you'd think someone had chipped in from 100 yards. I've never seen anything like it. And I would never, ever have wanted to be in his shoes.

But it can happen to the very best players. Ernie Els is one of the all-time greats, he's had a career that most people would kill for. But I've seen him go to pieces on the green, and not just any green. He did it at the 2016 Masters. He six-putted the 1st hole!

He's two feet away and he overshoots. Then he shrugs it off, goes to finish it and knocks it two feet past the hole again. And then he walks around, hits it for a third time and he still ends up two feet away. And you can see that he's got a wry grin on his face, but his shoulders are heaving and you can tell he's mad with himself. So he takes his time, gets his composure back and this time he misses by six inches. And it's all going wrong now, so he does that thing where you just reach out one handed and casually back-tap it in, but he misses that too! If that happened on your local crazy golf course and it was your first time ever playing crazy golf, your mates would rip the piss out of you. And that's Ernie Els! Golf is hard.

It doesn't matter if there's a billion people watching you or just one. When it goes wrong, it is absolutely brutal. Even if you're playing against someone, you don't wish it on them. It's like a bad injury in another sport; whoever they play for, you don't wish it on anyone.

When you're in it, it's like the fight or flight mechanism is going off in your head. Your brain just goes into emergency mode and you want to run away and hide. Sometimes you just want to hand the club to someone else and say, 'Please, just do it for me,' but you can't.

Have you ever watched a golfer in one of those moments? They always take their hat off and then put it back on again. Sometimes they do it several times. It's because their heart rate has gone through the roof and their head has started sweating.

You have to take a step back, mentally. The very worst thing you can do is what Ernie did. You can't just step up and quickly have another go. Take a step back. Mark your golf ball if you need to and then reset. Go through your processes again.

You know what you're doing, you know the hole. By this point, the damage has been done and it's not going to offer up any new surprises. Breathe. It's too easy to collapse and get overwhelmed. When you're in that state of mind, you probably wouldn't be able to do something as basic as make a cup of tea. I've had it before. Too many times. You have to fight your body and your mind and get it back on track.

I've seen so many top-end players, people who have won Majors, struggling to putt from three feet. And once something gets in your head, I'm telling you, it can get out of control. If you miss a short putt and you get one the same length again shortly afterwards, that hole shrinks. I promise you, that fucking hole gets smaller and smaller and if you miss that one too, the next is going to look like a keyhole.

Of course, the best way to avoid all this is to practise so much that it becomes less of a problem. And that's all it will ever be. Less of a problem. Look at Tiger Woods. The greatest golfer who has ever lived and he still focuses so much time on putting practice.

He's got his own drill. He gets on a practice green with a bag of balls and two golf tees. He sets himself up about four feet from the hole and he gets himself lined up. Then he puts those tees into the ground either side of the club face so it's like a little gate. And he will stand there, again and again and again, sticking the ball down, getting a feel for it.

He starts off one-handed because he doesn't need the control over the aim. He's got that little gate. He just wants the control over the power. And he'll do it again and again, maybe 20 or 30 times, trying to get that perfect flush connection and the perfect amount of power.

And then he'll use two hands. And then he'll set the whole thing up again, but from slightly further away. And after all that, even he isn't perfect. But he's a lot closer to perfection than he would have been if he hadn't warmed up.

I like to make sure that I stay on top of my set-up. It sounds mad, but it's really easy to lose your perspective and lose sight of what is actually straight. After two or three rounds, I can easily end up with a putt that's breaking left all the time. And I'm not above using a putting mirror. There are a few gadgets in golf that probably aren't worth your money, but I like the mirrors.

You throw it down on the putting green and loom over it, checking out your shape. I like to see my forearms lined up, making sure they're nice and square together, same with my shoulders and my hips. And you use it to build that repetition as often as you can until it becomes second nature.

And you need that sort of thing because you need some sort of feedback, you need to know you're doing it right, otherwise you just end up guessing. And then you'll just keep doing the wrong thing more and more.

The mirror is one of my favourite gadgets. I love the little putting gates you can get as well. You drop a ball down, maybe eight feet from the hole, and then you put a gate down about a foot away from the ball on the line to the hole. And then you just keep putting balls through it. If you've gone through the gate (and obviously you have to put the gate in the right place, taking account of any slope!) and the ball doesn't go down the hole, then your issue is power. So you can sit there and do it again and again and again and get that feeling in the way you hit the ball.

Learning how to read the green is key too. I always like to have a long walk around it, making sure I get nice and wide to see what the slopes are doing. Is it right to left or left to right? Is it up and down or down and up? You're researching, you're trying to give your brain as much information as possible to inform its decision.

But it's not just the geography, you've got to look out for weird stuff too. Is there a ridge in the green? They're bastards. Has anyone left their marker there? You don't want to get everything set up perfectly and then clip the side of someone's litter. Sometimes it's just as simple as spotting a leaf or a patch of sand, anything that could make the ball deviate. It's hard enough getting your own contribution right without having external factors throwing you off.

And then you've got to pick a line. If it's a long-distance putt, you need to have a line for the first half, something to give you a rough guide of where you putt it before you lay it in the lap of the gods.

After that, it's all just about speed. Controlling the speed is key. And that's why you spend all that time practising on the putting greens.

But there are other factors too. If you're really getting serious, you need to think about the type of grass you're playing on. And this is where it can get really out of hand. When you head to somewhere in the Middle East or in Asia, they sometimes have a grain on the grass. You can see light patches and dark patches.

That's a whole different ball game, that's a new headache. If you're putting down and it's shiny and light, the ball is moving twice as fast. If you're putting it into the dark grass, it's twice as slow. And that's a mind-fuck.

And that's just going up and down. If you go across it, it's even worse. So if you're looking at aiming to the left of the hole and the green is going the opposite way, you need to send it straight because it will hold against the line. Still with me?

It's just the type of grass they use, the way it leans into the sun. It affects everything. I always try to warn the amateurs about it. If you see dark, it's going to go slower. If you see shiny, it's going to go faster.

So there you go; if you haven't got enough to deal with already, you've got nature trying to stitch you up as well.

What you don't do, under any circumstances, is get yourself involved in someone else's nightmare. If the person you're playing golf with is in a mental tailspin, if their entire game is going down the plughole, here's what you do:

Shut the fuck up.

Just let them get on with it, let them do what they've got to do and stay the fuck out of their way.

No-one has ever tried to offer me advice in those moments and I would never try to do it to anyone else. That's the funny thing in professional golf. Unless you ask for help, no-one's going to suddenly offer it. And I like that.

After the round, it might be different. Professionals will usually share some tips and stuff like that, you might even pick up some good information that way. But when you're playing, there's nothing at all.

Amateurs playing with amateurs? That's a different matter entirely. I've seen amateur players freely giving out the worst advice you can imagine, just throwing out phrases they've heard without taking a really good look, the way a coach would do. You just hear people going, 'Keep your head down! Keep your head still!' Like it's going to fix everything. Keep your head down? Oh, really?

That's bad advice. Your head is going to move. It's going to go from side to side, it's got to move or you can't move your body properly. It's just shit advice.

If I was pushed to offer something, I'd just urge you to go back to your basics, check your set-up. Get yourself all matched up. If your shoulders are all over the place, you're going to struggle. If your forearms are all over the place, it's going to be hard work. Get straight, get square, get a good connection. That's the key.

The best putt I've ever hit was at the German Open in Cologne. It was on the 9th hole, a really difficult one. It's a really weird green, long and skinny, maybe 40 yards long with the hole right at the back. I've hit my second shot onto it, front left, and I remember thinking, 'Oh shit, this is a long putt.'

I walked up to the back of the hole, there was a big hospitality stand behind the green, and I had a good look at the green, trying to get a gauge on it. It was sloped, downhill and left to right, so it was a massive break over the better part of 70 feet, and if you hit it too hard it could easily pick up speed and end up in water off to the right.

I hit it and just thought, 'That looks all right.' But it was such a long distance. It seemed good on speed, it seemed to be breaking nicely, and three-quarters of the way along I'm thinking, 'This has got a chance …'

And it's gone straight in the hole. The crowd was surprised. Even I was surprised. I did some stupid celebration out of excitement and everyone was just laughing, it was a ridiculous putt. But through all of it I wasn't really thinking about getting it in the hole, I was thinking, 'Don't put it in the water!'

But the most important was that putt at Valderrama to finish my round and win a tournament. Just four feet and yet it's one of the biggest pressure shots I've ever taken.

The one thing you can't do is lose your temper. And I say that as someone who has lost his temper way too many times. I've thrown my putter away, I've smashed it into the ground, I've buried it into the mud. You see it all the time. But you've got to be careful with the timing. Remember that you're only allowed to go out with a certain number of clubs. There was a player once who broke his putter on the third hole and he had to do 15 more using his pitching wedge to get it down the hole!

If you are going to do that sort of thing, best to save it for afterwards. Though even then you have to be careful. There's a story I've heard about a golfer who had a really bad day out there and he marched into the clubhouse and tossed his putter on an open fire. Of course, he forgot that there was a rubber grip on it and they had to evacuate the whole place because of the smoke!

Some people have such a tough time with putting that they rip everything up and change their grip or opt for some really unorthodox, weird style.

After my time out of the game, I decided to try a new grip and see if that would help my putting game. I spoke to my coach and went for a grip called 'The Claw', which is a pretty funky, almost one-handed grip. I tried it out on the putting green in Dubai and I liked it, it worked well for short putting. And then I'm on the 5th, I've hit the fairway, I've landed my second shot to within three feet of the pin, feeling pretty good about myself, and my playing partner has rolled it in from 60 feet. And I've stood there and for some reason I've gripped the new grip and my brain has just gone. I thought, 'Oh no, I don't like this, not in a tournament, I don't like it!'

And I've fucking stood up and missed the shot. And then I nearly missed the next one for par. I had to revert back to my old grip. It can be really hard making the transition, it can really play on your mind.

Some people go even further than that and try things like the long putter. I've never understood that, it looks so uncomfortable.

Bernhard Langer was one of them – it looked like he'd whipped the pole out from a family-sized tent and was trying to putt with it.

There were the belly putter guys as well, who would use their torso to provide support, just wedging the top of the club under their gut. That got banned. I saw one player on the PGA putting one-handed; he held the club in his left hand and he sort of held his forearm with his right hand. You always wonder what happened to them to make them do something so different with their game.

But I do understand it. There's no hiding place with the putting game. If your tee shot is a bit off, you can get away with it. If your approach play isn't quite there, it's not the end of the world. But there's nowhere to hide on the green. You can't physically get away with putting badly. It's just another reason why this is such an extraordinary sport. People will literally try anything to get that ball in the hole.

Oh, and people often ask me if crazy golf can help your putting game. It did for Happy Gilmore, but he was a one-off. You're never going to have to putt through the blades of a windmill on the PGA Tour or bounce it off a fibreglass clown. There's a lot to be said for any activity that forces you to work on the control of your shot. But you've got to remember that it is a different surface, a different challenge and not really the same sort of thing at all.

For me, the best way to get better at putting is to spend more time practising on a putting green. Most amateur players don't do anything more than warm up on one. But serious practice can make all the difference.

Not that everyone agrees. I heard a rumour that a group of PGA Tour Americans decided to go and play a round of crazy golf and one of them brought his own putter and ball …

18

COMEBACK

After playing a grand total of one tournament in two long, injury-ravaged years, I had mixed feelings about finally making my comeback in late 2023. I was excited, of course I was. But I was nervous too. Not about my performance, but my hand.

The last time I'd tried to come back I injured myself again straightaway. What if that happened again? What if I found myself unable to grip a club properly by the end of the first round? As the big day got closer, I became increasingly anxious. When you're out for a long time, you can focus on that distant point in the future when it's all okay again. But the nearer you get, the more you think ... what if it isn't?

We flew out to Johannesburg in late November, five days before the start of the South African Open. As soon as I got to the golf course, I felt like I was back at home. It's been a long two years for me and Jodie, but it felt like this was the light at the end of the tunnel. I saw my coach, Jamie Gough – I'd barely seen him for two years and I'd been playing some of my best golf with him in 2021. I got three days of practice rounds in and my hand felt fine.

It was weird, I didn't feel like I'd been away. I just fell straight back into it. Of course, it helped that I'd been playing well for the last couple of weeks, practising on my own in Portugal. Hitting the ball really nicely. Getting my groove back.

And in no time at all, I was there. Name called, nice ripple of applause and out on to the first tee of the first day of a proper tournament. I stood there for a moment and took it all in. All that time waiting for this, all that time working for it, everything leading up to this one moment when I could make my return to the game I love. I stepped up. I swung. I connected.

I put the fucking thing in the rough. Horrible shot. The first of many. I hit the ball horrible all day long. I was all over the place. I got it out, got it on the green with a terrible pitch shot and then three-putted for a bogey. Welcome back. I ended the day with a 77. You can't win a tournament on the first day, but you can certainly fucking lose one.

In the past, that might have been enough to knock me to pieces straightaway. I've told you all about the tantrums and the sulks. And I'm not going to pretend that I wasn't pissed off here. But I took 15 minutes to give my head a wobble, I went out to the range and hit a few balls, and then I drew a line under it and I moved on.

The benefit of all that time out was having the chance to reevaluate myself. I could look at the sort of player I was and compare him with the sort of player I wanted to be. In the past, as you've seen, if I play bad golf I get a bad attitude. I just revert to that 'Oh fuck it' mentality and I go to pieces. A day like this in the past would have been followed by an evening of sulking and looking up flight prices to get me home before the weekend. But I wanted it to be different this time.

Had I played well? No, not even close. I was rusty. I wasn't at the level required. But the second day was an opportunity to get more reps in, to get more golf under my belt. I had to take that opportunity, not just sack it off because I'd had a bad day. So I said to myself, 'Go out there, we need a low one, just go for it and get a positive round under your belt.'

I ended up going round in 68 and I only missed the cut by a single shot. I got in the right place really quickly, made a couple of early birdies and I felt great. I was just, like, 'Hey! We're all right, we're good here!'

I probably pushed a little bit too hard, I put one in the water when I could have been more conservative, but I can't complain. You can never complain about being four under.

Golf is such a stupid game sometimes. It's such fine margins and sometimes you don't have to do a lot wrong to be four over or a lot right to be four under. Golf is hard and it's crazy and it can turn, either for you or against you. This was a day when it turned for me. Just not quite hard enough. Missing the cut by a single shot hurts, but I'd rather have that than miss the cut by ten.

But Jesus, did I feel the strain at the end of those two days. Two years out and then you're straight back into an eight and a half mile walk in 30 degree heat. I was absolutely knackered at the end of that, my feet were killing me. But, thankfully, my hands were not.

They'd held up to the test. I'd come through the first tournament and I was ready for the second one.

It was a four-and-a-half-hour drive to Leopard Creek for the Alfred Dunhill Championship. I hadn't been there since 2015 and I've already mentioned it's one of the most amazing courses in the world where you see all sorts of animals – monkeys, hippos, loads of them. Harley absolutely loved it, though she did start to complain that I was always having to go out and play golf instead of playing with her. 'Not again, Daddy!' she'd say.

As I've said, I've used the last two years to do some thinking and some talking. I've sought advice from people and one of the things that kept coming back was the work that I needed to do on my short game. Leopard Creek has some of the most perfect greens I've ever seen and so all of that practice paid off. I was putting brilliantly all day. It's just a shame that I still wasn't hitting the ball well enough elsewhere. I basically putted my way out of trouble and walked off with a possibly fortunate, but gratefully received 69.

A 72 on day two meant that I'd made the cut with plenty of room to spare.

But the scoreboard doesn't tell the whole story. I was actually five under on the 17th on the second round when I made a poor tee shot, got a bogey and then really fucked up the 18th. It's just a bastard of a hole. It's not a long par five, but it's an island green and it's really quirky. Even if you're hitting a wedge shot onto it from 100 yards, your heart rate goes through the roof. There's just so much that can go wrong.

And when I got to it, the wind had picked up. I hit a bad tee shot, then a bad second shot. I tried to go for the green with a six iron and I put the fucker in the water. Disaster. When I got to the drop zone to try to wedge it on, I was absolutely shitting my pants. One minute I'm in a position to win the fucking tournament and now I'm stood there thinking, 'I could make an eight here.' It's not unheard of, especially on this hole. Someone had made nine on it the day before.

I've gone from five under to being in danger of missing the cut and my brain is going full-blown panic stations. 'What the fuck are you doing? What the FUCK are you doing? Don't fucking hit this in the water too.'

Luckily, I didn't. The wedge shot was good and I knocked the putt in for a very welcome bogey, the best fucking bogey you'll ever see. I was through, and I was just happy to get off the golf course and get my card signed. What a fucker that hole is.

Of course, I got back to loads of texts from my friends asking me what on earth happened at the end. I was just like, 'You should have seen how bad it *could* have been!'

I never mind a bit of piss taking from my friends. They all know the game, they know how hard it is and how often it can bite you in the arse. It's when it comes from someone you don't really know that it pisses you right off. Like when someone says, 'How did you make a nine on that hole?' The traditional answer is to stare at them and say, 'Well … I missed the putt for an eight.' It's like a code when golfers have to tell people to fuck off.

Day three went to shit. I got found out. My putting was getting me out of trouble for the first two days, I could easily have missed the cut. I wasn't hitting the ball right and you can't do that on a course like Leopard Creek. It wasn't nerves, it wasn't fatigue, it wasn't the weather, it wasn't the course. It was me. I just didn't hit the ball well enough. I got a 78 and I deserved it.

I was pissed off. There was a lot of cursing, a lot of f-bombs. It's frustration. When you're competing at a high level and you're not up to it, you get angry with yourself. But again, the difference was the way that I was able to deal with it. I got it out of my system and said, 'Come on, man, it's all right. We'll have another crack at it on Sunday.'

I felt like I could, just as I did in Johannesburg, put it behind me and try to find the positives. It's another round of golf, it's another chance to iron out the problems. And I was able to recognise that making the cut on my second tournament after nearly two years out was a positive in itself. I couldn't have done that a few years ago. I got a 75. Not much better, but an improvement and a tie for 61st place and a little bit of prize money.

In amongst all of this, I got to see what Harley made of it all. This was the first time she'd really be conscious of what her dad did for a living and maybe that it wasn't a normal job.

She had an absolute blast, hanging out with the other golfer's children at the kids' club. She got to go on safari, so we had an amazing drive around looking for animals. And Jodie was loving it too. After such a difficult two years, it felt like we were back doing what we should be doing for a living. And then, before we'd had time to catch our breath, we were off to Mauritius.

I still didn't feel like I was at my best, but I could feel the improvement as the tournament went on. There wasn't any dramatic improvement, it wasn't like I just suddenly cracked it and was playing like Tiger Woods. It was just more and more shots that felt right. A bit more consistency with the connection, a bit more control. Like slowly turning up the heat in the house.

The wind was pretty strong in the early stages and that can make the longer holes very challenging. But I was hitting the ball so much better than I had been and was able to keep myself in contention. I finished one under on the first day and one under on the second day, easing myself into the cut without too much stress. On the Saturday, I was playing the best golf I'd played since coming back. I was striking that ball so well, I felt amazing.

And then I got a fucking seven on the 18th. That was really, really fucking irritating. Fucking golf, man. It drives me nuts.

It was a long par five into the wind. Usually you could hit the ball close to the green in two, wedge yourself on and have a decent chance of a birdie. But the wind was really up, too much for me to get close. So I went for a different approach. I laid it up onto the right side and then went to smash it over a hazard. I fell short and ended up in the rough. So I had to twat it out of the rough to get back into a decent position. And I don't know what the fuck happened, but I caught an absolute flyer. The grass must have got between the club and the ball because it came roaring out without any spin on it and it whistled off so far that it nearly went out of bounds. I chipped myself onto the green, but not in a good place at all and then it took me three putts to get the bastard down. Fuck.

FUCK! At that moment, I wanted to break every single club in the bag.

But again, I was able to feel that, push through it and then move on from it. I needed 15 minutes for the heat and the emotion to dissipate and then I calmed myself down. I was able to look back at three consecutive rounds of 71, three under par for the tournament and hitting the ball really, really well. Mostly.

I texted my caddie. I said, 'Fuck that finish. We'll come back and fuck this golf course up tomorrow.' I wanted to be persistent. As persistent as a drunk guy who's been booted out the pub and wants to get back in again at all costs. But it wasn't to be. I didn't realise it, but I wouldn't be coming back at all.

On the 16th, I'd had a really awkward lie on a slope. The ball was sat beneath me, so I had to sort of half squat and crouch to reach it. I'd say that it was 18 inches, maybe even two feet beneath my feet. But I dealt with it. I hit an absolutely filthy shot, a proper beauty, just to the edge of the green.

But as I've hit it, I've got myself in such an awkward position that I've nearly fallen down the slope into the bunker. I didn't feel anything go. I was fine and I didn't think anything of it and I went off to have that absolute nightmare on the 17th. But after the round I started feeling something. This pain in my lower back. By the evening I was really struggling, I was losing movement. I got Jodie to massage everything in an effort to loosen whatever it was up, my shoulders, my back, my lower back, my quads, my legs, but nothing seemed to work.

When I woke up for the final day, I couldn't move properly. I could barely put my own shoes and socks on. I went to see the physios and they did everything they could to try to sort it, but to no avail. I couldn't even make a back swing in slow motion, let alone wind up for a shot. They looked at me and said the words I'd been dreading in those final weeks: 'You're injured. You can't play today.'

All that fear came rushing back. Surely not again? Not another fucking injury. And what sort of injury would it be? I was out of a tournament when I could have finished in the top 20. How many more would I miss? Five? Ten? The whole season?

Even this withdrawal alone was a heavy blow. We'd spent so much money getting out to South Africa, we'd accumulated so many expenses. If you withdraw on the last day, you only get last place prize money. Even a conservative round on the fourth day would have got me ten times that much. The last three weeks of golf haven't earned me money, they've cost me.

But the money is the least of your worries. It's the points. You need to get enough points over the course of the season to qualify for the biggest events. You need points to retain your card. Is this withdrawal going to cost me entry to one of the Majors? To the big-money events at the end of the year? Or is it going to cost me my career by sending me back down the ladder where it will be even harder to get back up again?

In the past, this is how I would have been for weeks. Catastrophising. Letting my thoughts spin out of control. But I'm stronger now. I know that you have to look at the bigger picture. It was one event, there were plenty more to come. The physios were fairly sure that it was going to be okay. I hadn't felt anything go when I hit that shot, I hadn't felt it on the 17th or the 18th. It had only developed later in the day. They felt it was something that could be fixed with rest and anti-inflammatories. And so it proved.

I saw a specialist a couple of days later and they did a real golf-specific physio test for me, it was like getting a full MOT. They said it was just tightness. There are lots of weaker areas of my body due to the fact I just haven't played for ages. Put simply, my body wasn't ready for a sustained period of dramatic movement, not to mention all of that walking.

It's funny, you know. Some people don't think that golf is a real sport because it isn't physical enough, but the force that goes through your body is something else. You see the same sort of thing in baseball pitchers and cricket players. You're not running in like a fast bowler, but you're using the same muscles and you're trying to hit a ball as far as you can again and again and again.

I didn't want to take any chances. We cancelled our plans to come back to the UK for Christmas and chose to stay in Cape Town instead and prepare for the Middle East events. This made sense for a lot of reasons. Firstly, a long-haul flight isn't exactly ideal when you've just hurt your back. But it was also a chance to rest up away from any distractions. I love going back to London, I love catching up with my friends and my family. But Christmas in London would just be too much temptation. I'd be out boozing, I'd be over-eating, I'd be having way too much fun! Far better for me to stay out in the sunshine, resting and preparing myself for the next event.

It didn't take long for me to know that this was the right decision. The pain eased off quickly and I felt back to normal in a little over a week. As I write this, it's early January and I'm getting ready to get back out there and play again.

Jodie has been incredible. She's been a rock. She's always there to tell me not to panic, that it's all going to be okay.

She tells me to just chill out. And she's right. We were looking back over the last couple of years at Christmas and reflecting on it all. It hasn't been an easy two years, that's for sure. But it's given us so much. We've learned how to deal with things, we've grown in confidence. We've been taught life lessons and we're so much stronger now.

There have been so many occasions when I've wondered if I was ever going to play again. When I've wondered if I can even call myself a professional golfer anymore. I've done so much other stuff – the TV work, the BBQ work, the podcast – that I wouldn't blame people for thinking I'd retired months ago. Being able to get back out there and compete at a high level has been an incredible feeling.

I said to my caddie that I wanted to get back to where I was in 2016 because I know I can handle it now. I wasn't ready back then, but I've got the tools to deal with everything. I've got Jodie, I've got Harley, I've got experience, I've learned lessons. I want to get back up there and I want to stay there this time.

I'm armoured and resilient. I can handle the bad days, I can stop myself from losing my shit halfway round the golf course. I don't think I'll be throwing any more clubs up trees now. I made two cuts out of three and across those three tournaments I finished more rounds under par than over. Everything was trending in the right direction. Everything was heading towards better scores.

There's still a long way to go, there's still so much more I can improve, but I'm really pleased with what I achieved in my first month back. If I stay disciplined, there's nothing I can't achieve. That's all I've got to do. Keep focused, keep my head and keep improving.

It finally feels like we've arrived now. As a family. This is what we've been dreaming of for so long. This life. Not just playing golf, but travelling the world together. We've wanted to have fun and explore and try new things and, yeah, maybe win some golf tournaments along the way too.

I've proved that I'm fit enough to play golf at the highest level. I've proved that I'm good enough to play golf at the highest level. If I can just add some consistency now, I can get back up to the right end of the leaderboard and maybe even start winning some competitions. That's the ambition for 2024. That's the goal. And I mean to achieve it.

19

THOUGHTS FROM
THE 19TH HOLE

The funny thing about golf is that it's the sport that's seen as the most traditional, conservative, established game in the world, but it's probably the sport with the most uncertain future. The last few years have been really messy. We've seen an absolutely toxic split between the PGA and the new kid on the block, LIV Golf, and then a really awkward and massively unexpected 'merger' that just made people even angrier.

At some point, the organisations are going to have to find a way to work together, but it doesn't look likely right now. You never know what's around the corner, though. In January 2024, Rory McIlroy, who'd previously said that he'd rather retire than play for LIV, seemed to hold out an olive branch and Greg Norman, the CEO of LIV, seemed to accept it. Mind you, things change so quickly, it's probably best if I don't make any predictions.

If it was down to me, I'd have the PGA and the DP World Tours running from January to some point in the late summer and then have LIV Golf running a sort of IPL-style team competition, maybe with captains making selections, like a multi-team Ryder Cup. Or you could even have a draft system where teams are selected according to the players' rankings.

That way, both of the established tours would actually be strengthened by the arrival of LIV because players would want to get their tour rankings as high as possible in order to attract the best offer at the back end of the year. No-one would want to miss a single tournament!

That's the only way that I could see it working, but it's a bit of stretch because it doesn't seem like the different parties really want to work together right now.

But it has to change and LIV need it to change as much as anyone. For all the money that they've pumped into the sport, it doesn't really cut through to the mainstream. Remember how much the Ryder Cup dominated the back pages of the newspapers? Can you think of any LIV event that has done the same? Can you think of any LIV event that's made as much impact on the national consciousness as The Open? And you're reading a book about golf! You're literally the audience that they're looking for, but I bet you can't say (without looking) who's currently leading this season.

It will change eventually, it's a new business and these things take time. I'm sure The Open wasn't absolutely massive right from the start, but it would help if it didn't have to compete against the established events. People will eventually accept that LIV Golf is going to be here to stay, but there has to be some movement from both sides.

One of the most amazing things to me is that they spent all that money on players, all that money on branding and formatting and securing the golf courses, and then they let them go out there with such shit team names. The Crushers? The Range Goats? That's pretty poor. What makes your average golf fan decide to support a team called the Range Goats? What exactly are you supporting? The golfer there at the time? What happens when they leave? I don't get it.

Why not keep it simple? Have teams from different nations or regions? Get all the Australians together and get a rivalry going with the English. Get Jon Rahm to build a Spanish team. Let the Americans build teams from the east coast and the west coast and from the south and the north. I'd watch that.

Or maybe it will end up like Formula One and you'll have teams led by manufacturers. Maybe you'd have a Titleist team with everyone from that company lending their expertise to the cause, doing everything they can to push their golfers, or a Rolex team where everyone's got a stylish watch on. There's so many ways that you could build a bit of identity. So many better ways than calling them the Range Goats anyway.

It's funny, there were rumours a few years back that something was brewing, but no-one really took LIV seriously. The amount of money that was mentioned just seemed silly, people just laughed about it. And it was easy enough to say that you'd never join up before it became real. I think more than a few players dismissed it and then found themselves making a massive U-turn. There was too much money on the table to do anything else.

It caused a lot of controversy, and I totally understand why. There are some big issues in play. But look, as a golfer, you're guaranteed nothing in this world. No-one has a God-given right to earn money. We pay for our own coaching, we pay for our own travel, we pay to enter competitions. We're on our own and we have to look out for ourselves and our families. Because it can all end very quickly.

It doesn't matter what you've done, or what they say you've got the potential to do; if you get properly injured, you're properly fucked.

Look at me. One minute I'm in good form, playing my best golf in years, about to set off for the Middle East leg of the DP World Tour, the next minute I've played one tournament in just over two years. I'm not going to blame any professional sportsman for considering a big offer very carefully.

Think about what you do for a living. If someone came and offered you 20 times your salary to work fewer days somewhere else, are you really telling me that you wouldn't even think about it?

If you're Rory McIlroy or Tiger Woods and you've already made hundreds of millions from the sport, it's a very different situation. No amount of LIV money is going to make a real difference to your life. But for other players, the ones who are yet to make it big, the ones who won't ever make it big or the ones who made it big and are on the way back down … it's a huge call.

If you're Ian Poulter, who took a lot of stick when he joined up, you're heading towards your 50th birthday. You've won tournaments, you've played in copious Majors, you've done multiple Ryder Cups, you've been there, seen it, done it and someone else is selling T-shirts with your face on. Why would you say no to something that can secure an extremely comfortable future for your kids?

But you have to seriously consider the flipside too. The Majors and the Ryder Cup, they're the unbelievably special events that money can't buy. I could play the best round of golf ever on the LIV circuit, but it won't be anything compared with the experience of finishing in the top ten at The Open. My memories of a lifetime are all events that you might not be able to play if you go with LIV. You get some exemptions, of course, but for most people, it's a bridge burner.

People were ready to burn bridges, though. I love the DP World Tour and I loved my time on the PGA Tour too, but there are just so many tournaments. Name me any other sport whose new season starts just a few days after the old one ends.

So you've got a sport filled with burned-out professionals who haven't got any time out, who never get to switch off and recover, and then you offer them way more money to play fewer tournaments across a much shorter space of time. Of course people are going to say yes!

No-one is ever going to have a lot of sympathy for professional golfers who can win six figures in prize money for one good week at the office, and I get that, but this sport does take a toll. We're absolutely blessed to do this for a living. I had that little taste of reality lugging those bastard doors around and it stuck with me. I know how lucky I am.

But this is a tough sport. There's a cost on the body, with back injuries and shoulder injuries and, as I've discovered, thumb injuries too. There's a cost on the mind too. Again, not everyone is Tiger or Rory. Most of us know that if we don't perform, we don't retain our tour card and we don't get to play anymore. You get players who win tournaments, drop out of form, lose their card and you never hear of them again. It's brutal, and so if that sort of money gets offered up to players, you have to understand why they're going to go for it.

Look at the Jon Rahm deal. They're reported to have offered him $600 million to join up. That's an unbelievable amount of money. They must have a bottomless pot of it, it's completely crazy. How can you turn that down? He's friends with the former NFL player J. J. Watt and you probably saw his tweet about it.

'If this number is correct,' he said, 'I would have driven to Jon's house and used extreme physical force to ensure he signed that deal …'

And he's a former NFL man, they're not exactly on the poverty line.

Rahm's signing is an absolute game changer and it might be what's required to get everything else moving. I mean, don't get me wrong, the signings of Cam Smith and Dustin Johnson and Brooks Koepka, they were all massive, but this is even bigger.

There may be hidden benefits to all of this chaos, though. This sort of thing happened in cricket back in the 1970s when an Australian businessman called Kerry Packer started his own international cricket tournament and scooped up some of the biggest names in the game. It only lasted a couple of years, but some of what people dismissed as gimmicks are still in the game today, and it's unthinkable to imagine the sport without them. Packer's league had coloured kits and helmets, there were fielding restrictions and day/night games under the floodlights.

LIV Golf has 'shotgun starts' where every player starts at the same time on different holes, so it condenses the action down into a few hours rather than the whole day. That's not a bad idea. It makes it an easier event to watch on television, but it almost safeguards against unpredictable advantages. Sometimes you have days where the weather suddenly changes and anyone who started late is fucked. I got the benefit of a day like that at Birkdale once. I was in the first group out and I made a real mess of one of the holes. I was right on the cut limit and I figured I'd be in for a tense afternoon watching everyone go round, hoping that I'd just squeeze through. But the weather turned, the wind picked up and everyone had a nightmare. I ended up starting the next day in 20th place!

But while there are benefits to that sort of start, I think you lose something in the way the tension builds up. I love it when you're in the mix on the final day and you're in one of the last groups to go round. The atmosphere builds up as you get further around the course, you've got people cheering you onto every tee and it feels like you're walking into some sort of Roman amphitheatre when you get to the last. I love that drama, and I wouldn't want to lose that with shotgun starts. That's really special.

Maybe they could compromise, use the fairer starts on the first two days and then go back to the old way for the last two days?

I don't think the 54 holes gimmick (that's where LIV gets its name, by the way, it's the Roman numerals for 54) would really mean too much to most golfers. I mean, it's one less day at the office, but I don't know any golfer who has a problem with four days of tournament play. It's a proper test across what can be a variety of conditions. That bit doesn't need to change.

But they have to find a way through all of this nastiness or we'll never get anywhere. I wonder if part of the reason that Jon Rahm went over to LIV was the lack of transparency over the merger. I think the PGA lost a hell of a lot of trust over that because absolutely nobody saw it coming.

As far as I know, they didn't run that decision past any golfers at all. It blindsided everyone. And you've got to remember that the golfers who said no to LIV were the ones who got hurt the most by that. They must have been thinking, 'Hang on, I've backed you, I've turned down tens of millions of dollars for you and you've merged with them anyway?! I could have just signed with them and the end result would be the same!'

Poor Rory got absolutely stiffed. He was the figure-head of the resistance, he was out there fighting the fight for the PGA. And then they went and did that. The trust between the players and the tour will have taken a massive battering from that, make no mistake. And that's before you get into all the players who have fallen out with each other.

But something will happen at some point because it will just be too damaging for this to carry on. We've got three organisations all trying to straddle the same calendar. It only just worked when it was two. I think that in the next five years LIV Golf, the PGA Tour and the DP World Tour will have to sit down around a table and sort this out. Sponsors will lose interest because the audience will be so split and confused. If you're in the sport, it all makes sense because it's all you've ever known. But if you're new to it, where do you start? Competing tours that run on a near constant basis against each other with a third-party tour playing a different form of the game altogether that pays out millions to everyone. It's not exactly simple to explain how it works to kids.

One thing that might be easy to explain to kids, though, is this new virtual golf league that Rory and Tiger are setting up together. It was supposed to have started by now, but unfortunately there was a technical issue that forced the whole project to be delayed for a year, but it looks fascinating.

If you've ever played the virtual golf simulators that started popping up about 20 years ago, you'll know what it's all about. You smash a ball into a big canvas screen showing you a viewpoint of the course and a series of lasers track how hard you hit the ball, where you hit it and whether it was spinning or not, then the computer replicates the ball on the screen for you. Tiger and Rory have got this massive complex set up in Florida so that the whole thing will be indoors, with teams playing against each other on the screen and then turning around to do the putting on a series of custom-built greens inside the complex.

It's really fascinating and it's got a lot of interest already. ESPN have already agreed to screen it live and loads of players have said that they'll step up and get involved. I guess it's technically another competition attempting to move in on a crowded market, but it's not really the same as a whole new tour suddenly appearing.

For starters, the events only last two hours, but the big thing is the fact that you don't have to walk about for miles and miles. I've got flat feet, it would be perfect for me. I get off the golf course at the end of the day and my feet are absolutely killing me. Combine that with the air conditioning and I'll be all in!

The technology for the greens is incredible, as you can use it to recreate any green in the world. The surface can rise and fall to give you uphills, downhills and nasty left-to-right slopes. Some of the best putting coaches have them installed in their homes and it won't be long before the players start buying them up too. I guess it was only a matter of time before someone used the technology to make a game out of it.

If they can do all that and not make it tacky, it could be amazing. Because it's got to be great for the fans, hasn't it? You've got an indoor environment, so it could end up like the darts with everyone drinking and singing. But the fact that it's indoors makes it accessible to everyone, it means a nice comfy seat for everyone and, let's be honest, any sport that puts you in range of a good bar at all times is going to be pretty good in my book.

Two things would worry me. Firstly, that they don't get the format right. It's supposed to be teams against teams, which is fine, but I hope these are given better names and stronger identities than what we've seen in LIV. It's a difficult thing to find a concept that the players like as much as the supporters, so they'll need to make sure it's fair, but also that it's entertaining.

And then there's the technology. They've been held back by one big problem with the arena, but what if something happens during the game itself? What if the screens go blank or the internet goes down or there's a power outage? I'd be losing sleep over all of that. But it's really exciting, and I can't wait to see it up and running in 2025.

And if all of that isn't enough change for you, we're getting new golf balls too! We've spoken a lot in this book about driving the ball and how far people can hit it these days. Well, they're changing the balls to try to take a few yards off. And it has not gone down well with everyone …

It had to happen. We've spoken about the massive increase in distances earlier in the book and how very different the game is as a result. The simple truth is that we're hitting it so long these days that we're running out of golf course and there isn't the land available to extend them back to a competitive level.

The technology has improved so much that it's getting a bit silly. I've tried a few shots with old drivers. I took one round the Belfry once. The first drive, I hit it straight out of the middle, *whooosh*, I didn't see what all the fuss was about. But the next one, a very slight mis-hit, went fucking sideways. You've got to take power off to get any accuracy. The new clubs, in comparison, are amazing. They're so much more forgiving, so you can just wind up and throw everything at your shot without worrying that it's going to go off at a right angle. Combine a more forgiving club with a more professional player, a player who goes to the gym and works relentlessly on technique, and suddenly you've got obsolete golf courses. The power and the speed are insane.

Lots of amateur players are up in arms about this, saying that it's going to ruin their game, but I'm not so sure about that. There's a lot of mythology about how far people are hitting it in the amateur game. We're talking about taking 5 per cent of the distance off the ball, it's not massive. I don't think it's going to make much difference to those guys. And what's the pay-off? It would be better to ask what we lose if we *don't* do something.

Look at St Andrews. It's the greatest course in the world, but we're having days there where multiple players are going round 20 under. You can't play a Major on a course like that now, it looks daft.

Everywhere you go, your standard par four hole is completely neutralised by a big drive. You smash it off the tee, get within 100 yards of the green, chip it up and you've got a birdie chance. It's not supposed to be like that. It's supposed to be harder.

You've got a choice at the end of the day. Do you want to take all of these magnificent golf courses out of the tournaments and focus on the longer, often new-build courses around the world? Or do you want to do something to bring back some level of competitiveness? I want to be able to go to these courses and get properly tested.

So it's an uncertain future for this sport right now, but it doesn't have to be that way. We just need to make sure that the powers that be don't get sidetracked with irrelevant stuff like money and that they focus their attention on the health of the sport. Because it's not about the money really, is it? It's about the prestige. It's about testing yourself against the best and about winning these grand old tournaments.

Since the pandemic, more and more people have taken up the sport and that's great news. Local clubs are dropping their fussy rules and doing their best to be more welcoming. That's great news too. We just need the professional game to light the way for everyone, but right now it's all a bit gloomy. Too many tours, too many tournaments, not enough focus.

Yes, there's a lot of money sloshing around, but that's because there's a lot of people watching on television. The wages only look obscene because of the TV rights. It's not the golfers' fault that the TV stations are frantically trying to outbid each other. And where else would you want the money to go, but to the people out there hitting balls?

And if you think golfers earn too much, have a look at the PGA Commissioner Jay Monahan's pay packet. In 2022, his total compensation was $18.6 million. That's more than most of the golfers picked up!

We had it so sweet a few years ago, the fields were really strong, everyone knew where they stood and what was going on. We had such great strength in depth. And now it's all a bit of a mess. They have to try to get to grips with it all before it starts to turn people off.

That would be such a shame. It's such an incredible sport. It's hard, of course it is. The best things in life *are* hard. But it's hard for all of us. When you go out there on the golf course, you're facing the same challenges as any professional player. A bumpy green, a treacherous rough, a sudden gust of wind, a deceptively wide water feature. It's the same nightmare for all of us.

And that's not all. You're playing against your own worst enemy: yourself. Every golfer from the world's best to the world's newest is trying to keep their own brain under control, their own limbs aligned, their own heart rate down. Is there any other sport that makes such an impact on your mental stability?

But the greatest thing that we all share is that moment, first thing in the morning, when we step out onto the golf course and take a deep breath of fresh air. There are birds singing, there's dew on the grass, you've got a bag of clubs on your back and the world at your feet. And if you've planned your day properly, a bacon sandwich in your belly too.

Golf is hard. But it's worth it. I hope you enjoy it as much as I do.

ACKNOWLEDGEMENTS

I couldn't do what I do without the love of Jodie and Harley. They are everything to me.

Jodie is amazing. She has to put up with so much, but no-one ever sees it. She goes through the same emotions as me, she feels the same pain I feel, she works so hard for us but never gets any of the credit. She's the supporting rock of my career and of our family, and I love her completely.

I couldn't ask for a more wonderful daughter than Harley. To come off the golf course and see that little curly head bouncing up and down, a big grin on her face, running up to give me a cuddle … it's the greatest feeling in the world. But she's not allowed to read this until she's 18 because there are too many swear words …

I'd never have got this far without the support of my mum, my brother James, my sister Emily and, of course, Dad. When Dad passed away it must have been so hard for my mum, but she was unbelievable. She picked us all up and made sure we carried on. She never moaned or got upset about things in front of us; she's always been there for us. My family were always there for me; always available to drive me to tournaments. I'm blessed to have them.

I've been lucky enough to have worked with some incredible coaches over the years: Neil Jordan, Matt Johns, Alan Thompson, Hugh Marr and Jamie Gough were all fantastic. Thanks also go to Andy Williams and Middlesex County – I loved those days. The English Golf Union gave me the opportunity to play in some of the biggest amateur events in the world against some amazing players.

And I want to thank Shaun Reddin, my former manager too. I know it didn't end on the best possible terms, but without his belief and support I might still be on the building sites carrying those doors around. I hope you're well.

I want to thank Iain Macintosh for all of his help writing this book. I'm looking forward to getting back to the UK, sitting in a beer garden with him and putting the world to rights again. Jack Fogg is a fantastic literary agent and he's driven this project from start to finish. And thank you to Adam Humphrey and his brilliant team at HarperCollins for just being constantly awesome.

Finally, to everyone at North Mid, thank you for being the greatest golf club in the world. I've been there over 25 years, I've made so many friends, so many people there have looked after me as I've grown up. Wherever I am in the world, I can never wait to get back there.